"Al Ortolani's *Controlled Burn* blazes across the landscape of a poet's everyday life. Here you will find poems about everything from COVID to cabbage soup, teaching to retirement, pets to Peter Rabbit, grandparenting to buying boots, and always with the poet's signature witty, cool, and humane voice. Unlike many contemporary American poets who pad their work with fanciful excess, Ortolani's poems burn with a language so clear, concise, and under control that it makes room for new growth."

—Clint Margrave, author of *Visitor*

"A poet, a real poet, observes--he sees through what is in front of him all the way into what it means or what it *could* mean. "Nine Holes at the Elks Club" is such a poem, deriving rich meaning and possibility from a moment remembered from his childhood, watching his father playing golf alone in the morning at the Elks Club before work. The poem begins with the boy's father pulling him along in a golf cart, and it ends beautifully and poignantly:

> *Soon, the day would become too busy*
> *for a father and son, his wing-tipped spikes*
> *holding us to the earth.*

This is poetry, made (as real poetry is) from whatever is at hand, and finding meaning there through the eyes of (in this case) a watchful young boy who would grow up to be a fine poet."

—Patricia Traxler, author of *Paradise Notes*

Also by Al Ortolani:

Slow Stirring Spoon (chapbook) (High/Coo Press, 1981)

The Last Hippie of Camp 50 (Woodley Press, 1989)

Finding the Edge (Woodley Press, 2011)

Wren's House (Coal City Press, 2012)

Cooking Chili on the Day of the Dead (Aldrich Press, 2013)

Waving Mustard in Surrender

(New York Quarterly Books, 2014)

Francis Shoots Pool at Chubb's Bar (Spartan Press, 2015)

Paper Birds Don't Fly (New York Quarterly Books, 2015)

Ghost Sign ((co-authored), 39 West Press, 2016)

How Wally Lost His Thumb and the Boy Scouts Became Cannibals, (Spartan Press, 2018)

On the Chicopee Spur (New York Quarterly Books, 2018)

Hansel & Gretel Get the Word on the Street ((chapbook), Rattle Press, 2019)

Swimming Shelter: An Exercise in 100 Days of Poetry (Spartan Press, 2020)

The Taco Boat (New York Quarterly Books, 2022)

The Bull in the Ring (Meadowlark Books, 2023)

Controlled Burn

Poems by Al Ortolani

Spartan
Press

Spartan Press
Kansas City, Missouri

Spartan
Press

Copyright © Al Ortolani, 2024

First Edition: 1 3 5 7 9 10 8 6 4 2

ISBN: 978-1-958182-79-6

LCCN: 2024943250

Cover image: Jacque Allen Forsher

Title page image: Al Ortolani

Author photo: Stanley Cope

The author would like to thank the editors of these publications where some of these poems first appeared:

The American Journal of Poetry: "A Man on a Fast Horse," "Pink Birds," "Transistor Radio"

Anti-Heroin Chic: "Cricket Shoes," "The Poorest County in Kansas," "Would You Would You"

Eunoia Review: "Controlled Burn," "Grinding the Christmas Sausage," "Mountain Goats on a Highway West of Aspen," "Nine Holes at the Elks Club"

Front Porch Review: "First Chill," "Lunch at the Refugee Café,"

Hobo Camp Review: "Climbing the Tower at the Drive-In Theater"

I-70 Review: "A House in the Strip Pits," "First Horse"

Long Island Quarterly: "Hedge Apples," "No Phil Rizzuto"

Main Street Rag: "Otto's Alligator," "The Old Guy with a Pencil"

Midwest Quarterly: "In the Flint Hills Near Bazaar, Kansas," "Terminal Blend"

Missouri Haiku Project: "Planting Daffodils at the Dog Park,"

New York Quarterly: "Cross Town 1957," "Driving to the New York World's Fair"

New World Writing Quarterly: "Black Swans," "Garage Storage," "Losing a Ring," "Rehearsing the Winter Concert"

One Art: a journal of poetry: "Acorns on All Saint's Day," "Armadillos Sought for Leprosy Studies," "The Big Gray," "Entering the Auction Barn"

One Sentence Poems: "Delivering Groceries to the Blind Woman on First Street"

On the Seawall: "Cabbage Soup," "How I Became a Bird"

Poetry Bay: "Graduation Photo 1949"

Rattle: "Leaf Removal"

Rattle Poets Respond: "Reading William Stafford While the Russians Shell the Nuclear Reactor at Zaporizhzhia"

Table of Contents

The Lady Who Lost Her Teeth

American Socialist

Eating Tater Tots at the Jingo Diner

Utopian Gravy

squeeze

Terminal Blend

open screen,
the first chill whispers
to the marigolds

For Mike Holman,
Brother-in-Law, Builder,
Master of the Frisbee

And for my sister,
Dianna Holman, Teacher, Lover of
Chicken Train, Funniest
Woman in the World

Together

.

In memory—
Micheal Heffernan
Poet, Teacher, Man of Letters
1942-2024

Author's Note

Controlled Burn has been a bewildering collection to put together. The poems gave me the sense that I'd broken down in an old truck while traveling from one distant part of my brain to another. Post pandemic living has been this way for many of us, and my guess is that as history looks back over these years, it will judge our shared existential crises as one that swept us through an extreme mix of mental, if not, spiritual geographies. In that sense, I kept this collection together in a single volume, rather than dividing it into two or three slim volumes.

During the time span when *Controlled Burn* should have been hitting the press, I was distracted by bringing my first novel, *The Bull in the Ring,* to publication. It was a work in progress for too long not to see it through to the end. Since that time, *Controlled Burn* has resurfaced. Many of the poems had been stewing in my journal. As I reviewed my selections, I hesitated, wondering if my decision to keep its scope broad and rough-edged, or to take the machete to it. I decided to leave it as it is. Maybe I was tired. Maybe I preferred the unruly woods, the wilderness of weak and strong, thick with rabbit runs and thorny blackberries, rather than the cultivated suburban park.

My family and close friends are part of everything I write, especially my wife who knows me better than I know myself. Thank you, Sherri. You keep the kindling dry. I also want to thank Spartan Press and editor Jason Ryberg for holding the door open to whatever fire *Controlled Burn* can bring, and to Jacque Forsher for her painting *Delayed Flight*. Thank you again for your cover art. Your work warms with a fire all its own.

A special thanks to Timothy Green, Patricia Traxler. Michael Simms, and Clint Margrave for reading this collection and providing their cover comments. I'm honored to have you involved. As always, there's been a band of brothers in my life who are always with me in spirit. Here's to the Picasso Brothers, Bull Sluice, White Buffalo, Fitton Cave, Mr. X, and Terlingua, Texas.

—Al Ortolani. Laurie, Missouri, May 15, 2024

Controlled Burn

Leaf Removal

I listen to my wife on the phone
explaining to Leaf Removal Inc.
how we just can't
pick up the leaves anymore.
It's getting to that point she says
that we need someone, which really
isn't true because we could slide
down the hill on our heels, rake
the leaves into piles, douse them
with charcoal lighter, and set
them ablaze. Then we'd just need
a metal tined rake to lean on,
a little luck to keep the house
from going up in flames, and with
the garden hose uncoiled, nozzle
dribbling like a mouth, watch
last year turn to smoke,
a slip, an ass tumble. Instead,
two rabbits leap out of the leaves,
zig zagging ahead of the dog
who forever believes he's a hunter
with sharp white teeth and
the speed to stay stride for stride
with the memory of himself.

Controlled Burn

By late afternoon strong winds
pick up down the main lake channel.
I let the flames rest, cool to ash.
I wet them with the garden hose, coals
sizzling, gasping in the flood of water.
For my own fire, I down bottled beer,
watch the blackened scars
at the bottom of the hill for a wisp
of smoke, a wave of heat in the late sun.
The evening news is full of flames,
kindled from dead leaves and windfall.
It is difficult to hold back a fire.
Flames leap the pit, the scratched ring
I've raked to rock, to nothing.

November Morning

There's a change in the air, a bite
to the morning that edges the first
cup of coffee. Possibly, it just the silence
between the trees, the contraction
of membrane in the nose.
I'm guessing it is this, but as much
the sense of ending when all that has
been sliding from the tilt of summer
rests in the stillness of zero.
There's a chance of snow in the air,
a hollowness in the heart
which precludes the senses. Yesterday,
a racoon the size of a coyote crept
onto the neighbor's deck to eat the birdseed
that had fallen from the feeders.
He stood on his hind legs and hissed
when the glass door opened.
In the predawn light there is no difference
between city streets and fallow fields.

Leaving Lonesome Dove

I've told my students that reading
teaches us about the hardships we face
from the safety of our armchair.
(Something I'd read somewhere.)
Yesterday, I finished a good book
and I'm sorry it is done.
Now, it's just the two of us with
our hard covers and our paper blurbs.
I slide the book between my fingers,
massage the spine, as if working out
the knots in its muscle. Tonight,
with the book closed, the house is
simultaneously empty and full. When
my daughter drove off with her fiancée
in a packed U-Haul, walnut husks
split under its tires. She waved
the dog's paw through the window.

Cabbage Soup

How I Became a Bird

The birdwatcher, a Dr. Somebody,
led my father into the bedroom
to see his wife, a Dr. Someone Else.
She had turned her knee while stalking
a woodpecker in the strip pits.
The old couple were childless
unless you counted a whippet named Floyd.
I sat in my designated chair, a Windsor
of family note, kicking my legs,
behaving as I was warned to, watching
birds I couldn't name dart
from to limb to feeder.
I'd had no experience
with floor to ceiling picture windows,
the two chairs, the table with binoculars
and coffee mugs, the glass
squeegee-cleaned with a special blend
of vinegar and water. But I was
the fastest boy I knew. So, I ran towards
the birdbath, the fountain of hose water.
Thinking the window a wall of open air,
I leapt like an impala.

My father picked me up off the floor,
as Dr. Somebody asked Floyd
what species other than birds
flew into windows. He wiped the smudge
my nose had made off the glass
with his handkerchief, bemused, as if
taking notes for Audubon. He explained
through my tears how birds,
flying into what they thought

an open room, sometimes
knocked themselves out, or worse.
I was the first mammal he knew
to try the same. He searched my neck
for pin feathers. My father pressed
an ice cube to my head. Dr. Someone Else
hobbled in on her crutches with binoculars
and perched against the doorjamb.
Oh, it's a little child, she said.

Driving to the New York World's Fair

Small towns and historical markers
are circled in ballpoint. Scenic highways,
dots along a blue highway, darkened
in pencil by my mother. Dad never stops.
There's a broiler pan for pee in the third seat.
My brother has dropped cherry Fizzy
tablets in it. When the Plymouth breaks down
outside of a small Missouri town,
Dad leaves my mother
with my brother and sisters and takes me
down a hill through a stand of trees.
He says that a man and a boy
are less frightening than a man alone.
We stop at the first house.
Already, it is dusk.
Dad tells the lady behind the door
that we broke down on the highway.
Could we have some water? She weighs
our sweat, my Yankee ballcap,
my white Converse shoes.
She returns with a pitcher of ice water
and two small glasses. Dad explains
the water, the car, the radiator.
There's a bucket in the garage
and we fill it from the hose. Dad offers
the woman a dollar for the bucket.
The sun has angled towards the horizon.
Our car is filled with last light, with heat,
with sweating children. Mom holds a towel
in front of the baby's face to block the sun.
Dad layers athletic tape across the radiator,

fills the dry mouth from the new bucket.
We inch forward into town, not the one
circled on the map, but one we've never considered.
There's a 24-hour mechanic.
Mom buys hamburgers in the all-night diner.
There's air conditioning.
Dad sits on a folding chair outside the garage.
A whip-poor-will rakes the distance between us.
What's that? I ask about the welding iron, the pop
of flame under the hood. A rosary dangles
in the quiet between dad's fingers.
He says, some kind of bird.

Cross Town 1957

We had just entered NYC, maybe
off the New Jersey Turnpike.
I don't know. There was a tunnel,
exhaust fumes, traffic noise.
Dad, proud of his new Plymouth,
tried to negotiate cross town traffic
to Long Island. Although he was born
and raised in Huntington, he had
never driven Manhattan.
A Kansan for five years now,
he drove with his arm out, signaling
manually, at times, pointing lane changes.
We stopped mid-block by a park
with a statue and a loading zone,
with pigeons and a food cart,
with a jack hammer and a thousand voices
attached and unattached to faces.
Dad asked directions from a man with a hat
with a newspaper in an unbuttoned raincoat.
From my backseat vantage,
I remember a disheveled shirt, a narrow
pencil tie, the hurried vowels
on his tongue, like one of my NY uncles
with his here's-what-ya-gotta-do
before the bus arrives,
before the light changes, before the meteor hits.
He knew a better way, street to avenue to street,
making sure we understood the intersections,
the curve of the harbor, both the bridge
to take, and the bridge to avoid.
Dad eased his watch-my-fuckin-fender Plymouth

into traffic. Mom, like an anthropologist,
said the stranger was a perfect example
of New York attitude, of it's no big deal,
but you gotta know this. This stop. This go.
Dad shrugged.
Mom held my belt, lifted my sister to see
the Empire State Building.
I leaned out the car window.
High above me, birds
flew between the canyon walls, nests
who knows, somewhere up
between the street and the sky.

Nine Holes at the Elks Club

My father pulled me along with the cart,
the irons and woods rattling, leather socks
hooded like monk's cowls. I enjoyed playing
with the multi-colored Ts, sticking them
in the soft earth, but the balls themselves,
dimpled, glossed with promise, held the early
morning light. Dad gave me a cast-off, cut
and grass-stained, to put in my pocket, to roll
across the green while he lined up a putt.
He preferred the course before work,
the sun climbing, the dew untouched.
Soon, the day would become too busy
for a father and son, his wing-tipped spikes
      holding us to the earth.

Whooping Cough

Mom dropped the thermometer
on the kitchen table. The glass
shattered against the Formica. Pushing
the beads of mercury into a single
jelly, she took a dime from her purse
and showed us how we could
polish Lady Liberty like a mirror.
We took turns rubbing the dime,
oiling it with mercury, watching it shine.
Mom was wise to poison, but how
could she know what she didn't know?
She wiped the table with a washcloth,
dropped her dime back in her purse
where it shone among the pennies,
the nickels, the bus fare out of here.

First Horse

My father was a New Yorker, who brought us

to Kansas in the fifties. He bought a house
on a dusty lot next to a cornfield.
He used a baseball bat to sketch in the dirt
where we'd put a corral for our first horse.

He explained how we'd paint the barn
red like the barns in photographs. I sat
next to the make-believe feed trough
and dreamed about sugar cubes and apples.

Instead of a horse, there were three sisters,
the smallest of them rode on my shoulders,
kicking her heels against my chest.
I'd trot out of the invisible gate,

whinnying and tossing my head.
My sister had a congenital hip dislocation

and had to wear a brace for years.
In high school she became a cheerleader,
known to love horses,
especially palominos like Trigger, the one

Roy Rogers rode into television history.

Juicy Fruit Gum

The walk took me down Joplin Street
from the old Navy barracks, which had been
converted to married student housing.
It was a good mile to my grandmother's
and as straight as they say
a crow flies. My grandmother waited
nervously peering around the corner
of her porch for the first sign of me
coming up the road with my hands
in my pockets, past the row of rentals,
run down and slanted out of flush lines.
The residents my father said were poor
without a bucket to piss in.
They watched from their porches, frames
as bent as their lives. They worried me,
following with their eyes
the only distraction out of the usual traffic.
Old women, old men, metal chairs.
I whistled as best a four-year-old could
as if walking so far from home was just
another casual morning. That somehow
the poor would leave me alone if I
showed no fear—if I let them see that
I had a grandmother.
I learned years later that my father waited
one block west at each intersection
for me to pass. Amused by my decision
to walk to grandmother's,
he slipped me a stick of Juicy Fruit
for the tough times ahead.

Losing a Ring

My father blamed himself. My mother said
he should have listened. Who gives
a four-year-old a gold ring?
                              And that's how
it was left, like a tree ring on a stump,
like the ring of a hammer on a nail.

Today, I have a box, tucked with silver
quarters, pocketknives, and tired watches.
I dole them out to my grandchildren
as they reach an age
when time is more a hallway to another room,
than a four-year-old's circle within circles,

and sometimes after Sunday dinner,
the dishes dried, the pots and pans stacked
in a cabinet too small to hold them,
I bury my head in my hands and listen

to the empty house, the evening
coming down from the horizon, until sorrow
rings with wind, and like my mother,
my father,
there's nothing left to give.

Eight Ball in the Corner Pocket

My father, a dreamer, traded
a pitching machine for a pool table
He placed it in the center of the family room
which was originally a carport. Before
the pool table he had hoped hope to build a garage
with a workshop. a wall to hang bicycles,
rakes, shovels, pinup calendars. As money
permitted, the carport was walled in
with sheet rock and fake wood paneling,
the two of us a team. I rested
one end of sheet rock on my head,
then pressed it up to the rafters, arms shaking,
dad nailing fast, his hammer rhythmic,
a tap tap bang. The floor was tiled
over concrete, troweled with black glue,
then changed out when the next new baby came
for orange shag, luxurious, pile raked.
We played stripes and solids, learned
the irony of an eight-ball scratch.
When Dad developed Mennear's syndrome,
the spinning bank shots grew too much.
The green felt filled with laundry—
shirts, jeans, underwear,
endless baby clothes. I folded diapers
while rolling the eight ball
between piles of onesies. The corner pocket
caught diaper pins with safety latches:
pink ducks, blue rabbits, yellow chickens.

Gas as a Family History

I knew propane was connected to breakfast,
the blue flame that licked the frying pan
of bacon grease and sunny side eggs.
Grandmother had cooked on her mother's wood stove
until grandfather couldn't
keep the woodpile up any longer.

That was the story. Uncle Jim had been gassed
in World War One. Uncle Lee had driven
a tank with Patton in Africa. I wasn't
told much of his story. Grandmother said,
he ran out of gas and had to come home.

During the 50s, Cousin Joe topped off his gas tank
while on leave from the Navy, and was killed
in a wreck on Highway 69. To supplement
the GI Bill, my father worked at the Skelly
station for a boss named Sarge.
Sarge let me sit in the office and listen
to the bell ring when cars pulled up to the pumps.
I was supposed to come and get him
if the driver was a dish. I pictured my mother's
plates that she stacked in the drainer,
not the Blue Onion she kept behind glass,
but the ones with the knife scratches.

What I understood about gas stations
was that I was allowed one bottle of Coca Cola
each visit. Dad kept dimes in a piston paperweight.
The bottles hung by their necks in a red cooler.
If dad were out of dimes, Sarge would slip his hand
into his pocket and squeeze a rubber coin purse.

It was shaped like a mouth, the lips
would open, and there'd be a jingle of
nickels and dimes. Small change he called it.
I asked him once why the women's bathroom
was on the side of the building, and the men's
was just behind the rack of fan belts. Odd
that a woman might have to walk
through rain or snow just to pee.
Sarge said, no lady wanted a guy at a gas station
to know her private business.
We were gentlemen if nothing else.

Hedge Apples

The crazy woman next door said hedge apples
kept spiders away. My mother
preferred a commercial poison like Raid.
Cows bite hedge apples into chunks, and if swallowed,
they can choke them to death. As boys,
we threw them at each other in war games,
boys with good arms and boys who were targets
for the good arms.
It's a complicated world
we grow into, one where
hedge apples are good for little
except as bombs, and the souls of cows,
if they have one, are grilled
medium rare with cheese.

Once, we spent the better part of three days
throwing hedge apples at one another,
a Market Garden, a Bastogne,
our father's memories wrapped in secrets.
Probably, I go too far with this story,
stretch it like a bandolier of prayer beads
for those ground to hamburger,
for those whose memories are so sealed
they only bleed in sleep.
I know nothing of reincarnation,
but it is promising, the good arm

launching hedge apples, play acting
death scenes, giving strong last words
before dying on a news reel,
before rising like Lazarus. Maybe,
we are rehearsing, maybe reenacting,
to play out the violence in our brains
as children do in games.

Kerosene Violets

When my father took away
grandmother's car keys,
she called him a lousy bastard.
At the lunch table he found it a joke
how this sparrow of a woman
turned on him. But I'd seen her
like this once before when I visited
unannounced, her husband
a man I'd barely known
ignored the house for the garage.
She struck a match behind the screen,

tossed it into the sink
as he descended the stairs
to the brick patio he soaked
with kerosene each spring.
I backed out of the door
as I'd come, allowing her to
smolder as he drove away.
I stood on the porch watching traffic,
drivers lost in private conversations,
elbows on armrests, hands to chins
as if holding their mouths shut
or prying them open to scream.

Oldest Son

As a boy we had a dog die
about once a year. They ran loose,
each morning leaving the house,
returning at night from wherever
the neighborhood pack took them.
We knew each member of the pack by name,
by their owner's names,
by their speed, their thievery, their bark.
They chased cars on the county road,
and ate the poisoned meat
the farmers set out for rats.
Dogs were free. By that, I mean
we never paid for a puppy.
They came to us tumble deep
in cardboard boxes. Someone
always had a dog to give away.
A "Free" sign, once painted, was kept
in the garage next to the scrap lumber.
Mother handed me a shovel and the car keys.
She said, go before the others get home.
I used a towel, rubbery with Shinola.
I sunk the spade like my father did,
used my weight to lift the earth.

Cabbage Soup

My father kept a Rosary in his pocket.
He was known for giving away inexpensive
holy medals and pocket prayer beads.
At one point he handed out gold-colored
lapel pin doves. I wore one on my brown
corduroy for years. Maybe I still own it,
rolling around the bottom of a keepsake box.
Mom didn't go for all that. She didn't
even keep recipes of our favorite meals.
She wasn't stingy, but she held things inside
her head, rather than written on cards in a file.
I never met anyone who didn't like

her Sunday cabbage soup.
After dad passed away, we hoarded his rings,
his nine-dollar watches, his fake gold bracelets.
When mom's mind started to slip
and the kitchen grew impossible after Mass,
she forgot how to cook. I have a fragment
of a cabbage soup recipe which she talked me through.
It's vague and spontaneous like Kansas weather.
Like her, I've never written it down, but tweaked
and turned her spices into my own.

Grinding the Christmas Sausage

I.

The papa I knew, in the telling, grew chickens
and parakeets from eggs. He lost his boy Walter
to a midnight hit and run on Thanksgiving,
then the same night, tossed the priest
along with his god from the porch.

Today, I grind sausage in the garage in November.
The sons come to tell jokes, to drink Miller Lite, to watch
the Chiefs on the outdoor television. The old recipes

are doctored with crushed pepper, powdered garlic,
squeezed into store-bought casings.
By the fourth quarter, sausage links hang
like bandoliers, strung for revolution,
for Thanksgiving, for Christmas, then frozen
next to the ravioli from Big Mike's granddaughter.

II.

I crank an old press, found at a flea market, wheels,
blades, greased with olive oil, pork fat.

Today, I am the old man, the uncle at a reunion,
a second cousin once removed,
an usher at a Catholic funeral. Today,
there's a Dollar General in every neighborhood,
a street with a church, a church
below a viaduct.
Traffic thumps through morning mass.

My hands frame the Italian, the old words
nearly forgotten, liver-spotted, my eyes
like vowels in the window's reflection,

like dots in an ellipse to the moon.

III.

The truth at 5 a.m. is that the day begins
behind a thousand shut houses, a Catholic
altar, a bedroom light, a photograph
on a beige wall of children and grandchildren.

I am seldom without coffee,
without the crumb of tobacco on my lips.
This is what I know. Winter's face
is chilled, brittle with crow's feet. The surprise

is that I recognize myself so easily, a clock
with a battery on a nightstand, a glass of water,
pecan shells, a rosary.

IV.

There was always meant to be tomorrow,
time to adjust the contrast, to crop the photo.
How many generations will it take
to blur the face of the father, to lose
the grandfather, the great grandfather?

When the old ones walked down the gangway
to Ellis Island, I was already years
in the making, the lover of a lover of a lover,
a child turned old in a Kansas window,
my children and their children

in a city where the words metabolize like spit,
lopped to the tip of the tongue,
coughed up from deep in the throat,
battle axes and blades,
a loaf of warm bread, buttered, split.

Otto's Alligator

Pink Birds

On the top floor of Roth's Garment factory
is a skating rink. After school, teenagers sail
like loosened shipping labels across the wooden floor.
From my station behind the staple machine,

I watch them arrive with their skates in leather cases,
or tied by the shoelaces and slung over a shoulder.
Some I know from Geography or Easy Math, dropped off
by their mothers, their fathers in insurance or car sales

or at the foundry with the ladled steel.
Most skate with small agendas, cherry Cokes
sipped through the sun moats, the spiraled dust.
One girl comes for lessons, her cheeks

like pink birds as she rushes up the stairs
from her mother's Lincoln.
She is a dancer, a dancer on wheels, half
of the floor, reserved for her pirouette, her ciseaux.

Without doubt, she will make something of herself,
her hips swaying, her calves muscled, her eyes
riveted on the next move, on the choreography
above the sewing machines and the fabric cutters.

As the box boy, stapling for minimum wage,
I wonder if I'd already made myself into what
I am to become. Certainly, not a dancer, barely
a roller-skater, I staple boxes faster

than even Jonesy, who has worked the first floor
for ten years. My stack of ready-to-ship cardboard
stands to the top of the windows like a curtain.
With the Christmas rush, the boxes are parceled

across America, and no matter how I punch
the foot pedal, Mr. Woods, the floor clerk,
calls for more. The voice of the girl's skate-coach
echoes down the stairwell, spin leap smile.

Transistor Radio

My junior high band teacher
said my trumpet was a good instrument
even with the dents and the scabbed
alligator case, too good for where
I sat near last chair, hidden behind
the wooden music stand, next
to the window to the playground.
Once, during a sudden electrical storm,
a bolt of lightning shot into the band room
and nearly took our teacher's head.
The brass blew B flats, drums clattered.
One girl dropped her clarinet. Shut
the windows, the teacher said.

I left mine open a crack, suddenly
claustrophobic, the cool air
of the storm a tonic. My father
hired a private tutor for me,
and I walked each Thursday to a house
on Elm Street, a house well-sealed
with rote scales and valve oil.
There were storms that season,
low heavy clouds, rain drops
on the alligator case. On our all-brass
challenge day, I told the teacher
I'd forgotten my trumpet. I dropped
to last chair, back behind the kid
who smelled like liver and onions.

In high school, my father had been a stand-in
for the Long Island Symphony, attempted
a thin moustache like Harry James.

My mother had slapped a bass fiddle
and jammed with a college jazz band.
She hung out with guys
named Binx and Fat Arlo.
She said I was tone deaf.
My father said he was wasting
three dollars a week on lessons.
At night, I tuned my transistor radio
to WHB in Kansas City, buried it
between the pillow and my dead ear.

Rehearsing for the Winter Concert

In the trumpet section of the junior high school band,
the boys tongue quarter notes, more or less, in time.
They sit in two semi-circles behind shop-made wooden
music stands. Between songs, one eighth grader throws
his pocketknife into the wood. Sometimes it sticks.
Usually, it clatters to the floor at his feet.
The band director fails to hear the whack

of the knife. He's focused on the two rows
of clarinets to his right, hoping to avoid the frequent
squawk of a poorly mouthed reed. The loveliest girls
in the school play silver flutes. They perch in a row
in front of the bandstand. Near the instrument closet,
behind the trombones and the single sousaphone,
the drums are in disarray, clicking their sticks,
tapping rims instead of skins. All snares, not a single
bass since mononucleosis hit. The director
is a patient man. He only raises his voice to the trumpets,
who dodge knives and squeeze spit valves, or
to the drummers who confuse their sticks for rapiers.
The first chair saxophonist in horned rimmed glasses

squeezes vibration from his alto with pubescent verve.
Somehow songs like Sentimental Journey
emerge recognizable to the parents on concert night.
Their memories fill in the gaps with big bands,
how they loved to swing at roadhouses to Bugle Boy,
when chaos wore a uniform, and the trumpets
flashed from the stage like an assembly line
for brass shell casings, and the solo drummer
banged out battles to which they could dance.

Black Swans

Walking through my favorite park,
the one with ducks and two
black swans, I was met
by boys from the Catholic school.
I knew them from first communion,
from little league baseball.

They told me I could either jump
in the lake, or they'd throw me.
I tried to walk away, but the loudest
grabbed the back of my pants and jerked
my underwear. Ragged they called it.
My underwear was new, just
taken from the Sears package.

I thought of my mother, searching
the catalogue for bargains
to keep her children presentable.
Now, they were torn, elastic band
ripped into a handle. I was embarrassed
as much for her as for myself.
I scanned their eyes for the joke of it,
for baseball and sunflower seeds,
for the wafer that would have tasted better
with salsa. I noticed Paul, my teammate
from Meadow Gold. His expression
was flat, curious like a first time
executioner.

I stepped into the lake, rather than
get tossed onto the rocks,
arms raised, fists
mute, rather than bloodying noses.

I walked into the lake
and kept walking, the water rising
up to the armpits of my new shirt.
I heard the Catholic boys laughing,
then yelling for me to come back.
It was over, they said. But it wasn't
over until my mother looked up
from the catalogue, and saw me
sneaking in from the garage.
I waded and dogpaddled to the opposite
bank, never turning around, kept on
until the swans parted and closed
between us. No one loves a coward,
except a mother,
and that is where the pain floats.

New clothes came once a year
before the school bell rang. She wanted
me fresh like celery when it snaps.

Otto's Alligator

Otto saw what most of us didn't
like the alligator in the Little Woods,
hidden in the creek behind our street.
Our parents said not to believe
what Otto couldn't prove. As an orphan,
adopted after the war, he struggled
to hide his accent. His eight ball

improvisations towards friendship.
He discovered magical bananas
in a farmer's tree, told the boys
they were poisoned like the strychnine
that killed our dogs last summer.
He filled his handlebars with gasoline
so he could shoot flames
around the block like a jet fighter.
He rubbed poison ivy on his genitals
on a dare about immunity.
The flames burned his legs to blisters.
The combination left him bedridden, stinking
of barbecue and calamine.
He tested the thickness of ice
by walking into the center of the cow pond
and jumping up and down. He dug
a hole in his backyard
for us to sit and talk. It was
so deep we could stand
and not see over the top.
All this was well documented.

My parents declared Otto off limits.
The boys made up rhymes
about his uncircumcised penis,
sang them on the street outside his house.
One Saturday my mother read
in the paper that an alligator
had been captured by the dog catcher.
She asked if this was Otto's alligator.
I led an expedition to pick the bananas
from the house behind the cornfield—
which it turned out were walnut leaves
bright with affliction.

In high school Otto flat-topped his hair,
lifted weights, played football.
Never spoke of alligators.
The Church claimed Otto's
overdose accidental
so he could receive final sacraments.
The priest swung a censer on a chain.
Incense hung in the apse. The entire school
sang with the voice of a rose-colored choir.
I'd never heard such a thing.

Singing at Christmas

We drank the little money we had
in the alley between the Presbyterian Church
and the law office, sheltered from December
by bricks, the iron fire escape
where we downed a six pack, chugging
as they said, for affect, before
we had to move on, before
a neighbor caught us
who knew our fathers. Now, that we'd
quit basketball, our evenings were
free to explore our anger
at the injustice of talent. The city
had built small red houses for bell ringers
to sit out of the weather. Old women
and old men who volunteered
to lean from single windows, above
the metal cauldron of spare change.
I leaned on the windowsill,
singing the one about the Drummer Boy.
The bell ringer appeared embarrassed, maybe
on to my diversion. I squeezed my hand
under the wire mesh
and slipped two dollars from the pot.
We walked back to the bar
for Falstaff. The beer colder
which was good, but the unforgiving wind
rattled the silver bells, the plastic Jesus star.
We stuck to the alley walking home,
the Christmas air freezing tire tracks
in the slush. I'm sure my song
was flat. No voice to speak of.

Would You Would You

If your friends jumped from a bridge…
The answer of course was yes,
jump, always jump, arms and legs flailing
into the sky without a moon.
The water below, below the bridge,
below the moonless sky, split by
a stone, the guess of depth.
Finally, a silhouette
on a bridge alone, standing, turning
the truth. Alone on the railing,
with the truth, the bitch of the truth,
not knowing the leap, the splash,
all the while the accusations from downriver
rising like a nation,
up from the muddy river, the voices
of ducks, carp, and cottonmouths.

Climbing the Tower at the Drive-In Theater

It was a long way to the top,
the wooden ladder nailed inside
the tower, two by four rungs still tight,
still defying gravity. I followed
you up, not because you were my boss,
the soon to be projectionist,
but for the adrenaline of a climb
so steep I'd pitch over backwards.
I climbed above the expanse of farmland
spread in a grid of hedgerows,
above the lives tucked into small houses
below mercury lights, above
the semi-circles of cars facing the screen,
speakers hanging inside windows,
windshields dark like sun-glassed eyes.
We toed as near the edge as we could brave.
Hollywood played across the screen, a flickering
dream of John Wayne, of Maureen O'Hara.
No one can see us, you said, our silhouette
lost in the night above the projectionist's beam,
shifting, rolling with each change of scene,
a magic act lit by a carbon filament
by a man in a small room through a small window,
film cannisters stacked along the wall,
whiskey bottles ratted behind the shelves,
behind the coffee cans of nuts and bolts
and spent carbon. A hundred feet below
sat the ticket booth in the driveway. A girl
I knew I could love perched on a stool,
taking cash, handing tickets to the manager,
who in turn passed them through the window

of a Chrysler or a Buick. I couldn't tell.
Soon I'd relieve him, sit with this girl
I could fall for. We signed our names
on the wall with pencil, concave on the mortar
between the bricks, where we assumed
they'd last beyond our time, beyond
the few hours we had, like the movie
below the tower I'd climbed, the two of us
where no one could see
our nervous hands, our fear of love
when the credits played, when at two a.m.
the last Chevy rolled out of the gate.

Stacking Dishes at the Lipstick Hotel

The head dishwasher smoked like a kid with a plan,
flicking ashes, picking tobacco
off his tongue, explaining
his next best job, how this
was nothing
compared to selling cars.

In the evening, after the kitchen closed,
we were left alone with supper's
stock pots and room service trays.
We played a game with coffee cups,
pictured the women
who left lipstick
on the cups.
We judged
the color, the full lips.
We took liberties,
imagined one of them the call girl
rumored on the 5th floor.

We kept the water hot, scalding, wore
rubber gloves, scrubbed fast
with nylon bristles, polished
with steel wool. With the sink empty,
we cleaned the drain trap, smacked free
the beans and pork, the gristle into the trash.
We dried, stacked pots,
dishes, tumblers, coffee carafes.

Tomorrow needed a start fresh.
The cooks
arrived before the sun, maybe
as the call girl was closing her door.
I owned a motorcycle.
Home in minutes. Studied algebra
to stay clear of Vietnam.

The head dishwasher waited

for the police to pick him up. He was
witness to something protected.
Some nights I waited with him.
He snuffed his cigarettes

in a coffee can, kept
his eye on the corner, the neon
Open
above the bar. He never talked
about the names he could name.
I could stack dishes, keep
my mouth shut. Happy
with a motorcycle that went
nowhere special.

Delivering Groceries to the Blind Woman
on First Street

She listened
as if sound could tell
how I stacked her cans,
green beans on one shelf,
fruit cocktail on the other,
the drawer
with the can opener
to the right of the sink,
to the left of trust,

dove-tailed between
Jesus and the tea bags.

Driving to the Dairy Queen on a Country Road
We Play Chicken with an Oncoming Train

The train is just
across the bridge,
not yet out of the trees.
I stop the car on the tracks,
a dumb move.
The diesel horn
swallows the fields.
Out of time, still
she smiles, draws her
shoulders in, arms
folded across her breasts.
Nothing below the waist
              the rule.
        One kiss.
The diesel horn. I turn
the ignition. The starter
grinds, the engine floods.
The starter
a mobius whirl.
I pump the gas, imagine
the two of us

dead in a Chevrolet
worth two hundred dollars.
A farmer, coming up from behind
with chicken crates,
COOP bound,
bumps us off the tracks,
a lurch,
a hen squawk. The train
screams between us,

the engineer pumping his fist
from the window. Fury
in his knuckles. His face
a Churchill caricature.
The car rolls off the track bed. I pop

the clutch in first, the engine
ignites. Pistons. Valves.
I smile at her across the seat
like we've beaten our beige destiny
all Dairy Queen and milk shakes.

Changing the Marquee at the Cinema Theater

For K

I loved how you sat in my car
when the top was down, my ladder
extended out above the sidewalk,
the traffic on Broadway slowing
to see what from Hollywood was coming soon.
I knew what was in your heart
as I sorted the plastic letters, carried
them carefully up into the sky
into the lights. Sometimes I'd spell
words wrong just to make you laugh.

Jamie in the Air

Brother, when you climbed
the crane near Centennial Street,
you left Mike and Dana
on the controls. Not smart.
As you inched towards the top
where the boom rounded off to blue air,
one of them gave the lever
a tug, and the boom twitched
enough for you to be thrown
some said fifty feet
to the pavement. Dana described
the sound of peaches inside a burlap bag.
Mike lifted his shirt to his face.

I wanted to ask what
you hoped to see, riding
on the topmost steel. Was it
an ocean of cornfields?
A feather of a hawk slipped
from a tailspin? And in falling
was there time for sightseeing?
For Jesus? For Lazarus?
Or just a rush of wind?

You lifted yourself from the mud
and began to limp home.
Skull bleeding. Arms pretzel bent.
Mike in tears, Dana embracing air.
You made your way up Ohio Street.
Bicycles circled, Dana and Mike
at your side shouting survival.

I waited with my baseball glove,
newly oiled, an older brother
with a ball in the pocket.
Dad would have killed you
if you hadn't fallen so far.

The Summer of Noodles

I read a spam subject line today
something like eight body stretches
you can do from your chair.
With my eyesight being
what it is, I misread it as
eight body searches.
It gave me pause, wondering what
I needed to search
on a Tuesday afternoon in 2022

that I hadn't discovered,
let's say, in 1967, during
the Summer of Love, which,
of course, I missed, due largely
to my youth, and that I was
living in a small town in Kansas
where love was something that boys
mentioned to no one except
their mother on Mother's Day.
Mary Evans was my biology
lab partner. We shared two chairs
next to the Bunsen burner.
We never stretched, and certainly
never searched. That was

when I read an article at the dentist's
about the Summer of Love.
I thought about it throughout
the next semester, still in the
same chair, but next to
Dirty Bill, another 12th grader
trying to secure

his 10th grade science credit.
Dirty Bill and I stretched biology
for entertainment, stamens
and pistols made us giggle.
We were sent to the hall during
a slide show on meiosis.

We passed with Ds, adept at little
except striking matches. Bill joined
the Marines after graduation.
I enrolled in Intro to Poetry, taught
by a graduate assistant from California.
She didn't take roll, taught me
to pronounce Yeats correctly.
                              I wrote
letters to Bill in country, sent him
a box of Girl Scout cookies.
My letters were stretched
with Beat imitations. His answers
were haiku with a new vocabulary—
a mortar round in the history
of the English language.
I tipped a glass to Bill
on my 18th birthday.

I didn't pledge much of anything,
pretended to like Irish tobacco,
read some of Ulysses, stretched
my 2-S deferment
into a search for Thai noodles.

The Summer I Was Introduced to the Lord of the Rings I Quit the Job that Was Supposed to Keep Me Out of Vietnam

I shoplifted a carved briar pipe from the news store next
    to the Cozy Theater.
Out of guilt I paid too much for a can of Irish tobacco
    which bit

my tongue until about halfway through The Fellowship
    of the Ring.
I read outside my parent's house under a tree my brother
    planted

for a favorite dog that had chased a semi. I learned to
    blow smoke rings
in The Two Towers just after Gandalf disappeared in his
    fight

with the Balrog. It devastated me, the Fellowship without
    a leader.
Middle Earth without a mentor. I had work at the Municipal
    Pool.

My job was to wade into the low end and sweep
all that was loose on the bottom into the drain below the
    high board,

then dive twelve feet to the bottom, lift the metal grate,
and clean out the drain sludge, surfacing for air with
    handfuls of hair.

At six a.m. a chill hung across the water. Rain clouds
built on the horizon above Catalpa Street. Thunder
    rumbled.

I thought of Gandalf lost in the depths of Moria, Frodo
    in tears.
I dropped my broom, shook the chlorinated water out
    of my ears.

In the bathhouse Billy Devlin was spraying the shower
    floor
with a garden hose. I freed my Western Flyer from the
    bike rack

and pedaled up the sidewalk past the GAR cannon, Civil
    War brass
the color of mud. My boss yelled my name from behind
    the chain link.

He was a family friend, a good man without imagination,
    a retired
offensive line coach without a whistle.

My draft card was in my billfold. Without college, my
    2-S deferment
would change to 1-A. My mother and father were teachers
    with five kids.

They couldn't afford to pay my tuition. I lived at home,
chose to be an English major because they insisted there
    was no future in it.

I smoked my pipe as my chainguard rattled across the
   brick streets.
The Return of the King dogeared in my bike bag.

I was greeted by paperboys tossing headlines of the Tet
   Offensive.

As a Teacher, I Painted Houses

to stay on top of the bills. I was passed
word of mouth among the widows
at the country club. On rainy mornings,

I took my brush to a screened-in porch,
on occasion, down a shadowed hallway
into a bedroom, lit only by one light
from a table next to an armchair, the house
gurgling rain in the gutters.

I was jealous of the quiet simplicity,
the widow's attachment to the rotary phone,
the single lamp, a book
creased at the spine, held open to the page
by the weight of what had been read.

Some mornings I was served coffee
from a tray with a sugar bowl
and a small creamer of milk. Sometimes
a napkin and a cookie. We talked
about the photographs on the wall,

or the rain at the windowsill,
or why the room hadn't been
painted in twenty years.

The Poorest County in Kansas

I built my daughters a rabbit hutch,
scrapped together from scabbed lumber
along the wall of the garage. I nailed
them with sixteen penny nails from the bottom
of my toolbox, and then, tacked the roof
with eights from broken pickets in the burn pile.
Many I had to unbend with my hammer,
tapping them on a brick until they resembled
the straight lines they once held.
Chicken wire and steel cloth were a problem.
The hardware store was closed on Easter,
the churches pew-filled, the shops shut
on the bluest of Blue Sundays.
The rabbits, one white, one black,
had arrived that morning
in a cardboard box, nesting in a gym towel.
I drove the alley in my pickup truck,
hunting cast off wire. Finally,
behind a row of duplexes, picked over
for copper tubing and galvanized steel,
I found a small roll
of garden fencing, saved from rust
by the angle of a fallen roof. I doubled
the wire on the bottom to keep the rabbit's
feet from falling through the gaps,
eyeing enough space for their pellets
to drop into the berm they'd build
throughout the spring and summer.
When it cooled in autumn, I raked them
into the tomato bed, behind the crepe myrtle,
back where the paint is peeling, where
even rabbit droppings cool.

Turning a Year Older, I Receive
an Email from Palmer

We share the same birthday.
As boys, we drifted on inner tubes
and discussed 9th grade tits like veterans.
A black swan from the city lake
swam nearby. He was thought lost
by Parks and Recreation,
the victim of dog or prank. We knew more
about swans than girls. We kept
both secret, the grand expanse of wings,

the curve of neck, stabbing the mirror
for perch. We were free that summer
with our 50 cent inner tubes, over-pumped
by Old Man Tony into odd bulging shapes.
A few years later, we cold camped
in the Sangre de Christos, sucking
lemon drops, watching a young bear

overturn our campsite.
At some point, as Eagle Scouts
we tied a few knots.
The girls became women. The black swan
left a silver crease in the water, and the bear
grew old on our supper. I wonder today
what we did with the inner tubes.
We bought so many.

The Lady Who Lost Her Teeth

Do Not Swallow

This morning I brushed
my teeth with Cortisone.
I thought the tube
said Colgate. Without
my glasses, it was
an honest mistake. We are
Crest people, so I was
surprised by the new
brand in the travel tube. I suppose
it could have been worse.
Possibly, I could have
failed to notice the distinct
change in taste or the lack
of spit foam. The small print
read to avoid direct
contact with the rectum,
which gave me pause, since
I'm seldom so florid.
If swallowed, I should
call poison control
immediately. There
was even a phone number,
which I chose to ignore
since I felt the itch of this poem,
surfacing like a tick bite
or a poison ivy rash.
As a frame of reference
for any who have been stung
by a bee on an upper canine,

Cortisone has a bland flavor,
not as salty as Playdough,
less soluble than Crayola.
It's a bit like Styrofoam.

The Lady Who Lost Her Teeth

Old lady Monroe, Pearl
to her friends, wraps her
dentures in Kleenex
before going to bed. She
hides them where they will
be safe come morning.
Her house, locked tight
at the bottom of a dead end
off Broadway, is free
of visitors. All except

the mailman, and the boy
who cuts the grass. Both
have full sets of white teeth,
and except for the occasional
glass of refrigerator water, they
never come in the house.
Miss Monroe keeps
a steady retinue of ghosts
parading from her past.
Some are pranksters, like
her brother Emil, who once
hid her favorite Effanbee doll
in a well bucket. Another

is Adelaide Tuft, a school
girl rival, who stole
her first and only romantic
inclination. Miss Monroe
is cordial to them all.

She keeps a plate of ginger snaps
covered in wax paper
on the counter by the stove.
Each morning, a few cookies
are gone, some only partially
nibbled, and set back
on the plate. She knows

her teeth are well hidden,
not even the clever Emil
or the spiteful Addie Tuft
can find them. Some mornings
she cannot locate them herself,
and then she begins to worry

a little about her brain,
but mostly about the cookies
and her lack of manners,
when over coffee, she gums
them to nothing.

Peter Rabbit in Rehab

October ends
with a rabbit foot on
a chain, a keychain
of twirling leaves.
Nothing moves
except the spinning
on Farmer McGregor's
finger. Peter Rabbit

is weekly in rehab
with a prosthesis, dogs
in the waiting room
leafing garden magazines,
watching the door
for his release. Peter
is slower today
than he was yesterday.
He supposes he'll be slower
tomorrow. Without
his lucky foot, Peter
is just an old man
with yellow tennis balls
on his walker. No leaping.
No sudden turns
under the hedge. He needs

Beatrix Potter to turn
the page, to illustrate
an escape past

the vending machines
into the parking lot,
through the ornamental shrubs,
the spitting sprinklers, then home
past McGregor's carrots.
Yes. It was always the carrots.

.

A House in the Strip Pits

At night a racoon visited us, he would
rattle the trash bags, rip through the thin plastic.
If the back door was open, we stood
in the dark kitchen and watched him through the screen,
unloading tin cans, lunch meat packages,

a Tai Chi of chicken bones. Mornings
I slipped on my diesel-drenched jeans
for work with the road crew. A brown recluse
bit me on the knee. As I rolled up my pant leg,
he dropped to the floor, his violin
a solo from backstage.
We discovered spiders in every corner,
an orchestra under the bed, the cabinets, in our shoes.
We fogged the house, threatened the landlord,

broke our lease, and moved to a duplex
near the railroad tracks. Instead of a racoon
we watched the trains hitching boxcars.
We seldom slept the night, rising with horn blasts,
with wheels screeching, with tons of steel
slamming into tons of steel. That November

our daughter was born. She was smaller
than a loaf of bread. She slept beside us
in the family bassinet. We watched her
more than the raccoon, listened
for her through the trains.
We wrapped her in a pink blanket,
balanced a small hat on her head.

Full Court Press

The superintendent showed me
the gym where I'd coach basketball,
two baskets, a game clock, a short stack
of bleachers. It didn't matter that
I'd never played except
when I was cut from tryouts in 8th grade.
Rural school boards can't be picky.
I knew some of the rules: two guards,
two forwards, one center, all positioned
in gradients of height. I was still in college,
married with a baby daughter.
Graduation boxed in the base line.
All offense would be crushed by the press,
and I'd have to join with English
teachers everywhere, hustling for jobs,
certainly, to drive the school bus where
poetry and fiction met in locker rooms.
My daughter needed three meals a day.
I needed to step out from behind my wall
of books and blow a whistle, planning,
practices for a game I didn't understand.
Before leaving campus, I visited
the library one last time, searched the stacks
for coaching manuals and another
on the identification of cows and chickens.
I needed a car that started in winter
and someone to call when it didn't,
the three of us hub deep in snow
on a stranger's forty acres

The English Teacher Buys a Pair
of Cowboy Boots

I bought a pair of cowboy boots that I
couldn't afford because I needed to boost
the Wild West in me. Nothing changed, except
on those rare moments when I leaned back
with my legs extended, feet raised to the lip
of my desk, having shot the eye out of a
term paper, or, when I caught myself
in a reflection at the 311 Club, my boots
dark with purpose in the doorway. I could
have been dusting off my black hat, rather
than hesitating before taking the next step
towards the woman at the end of the bar
a long ride across Kansas.
The old gunslinger joked about dying
with his boots on, not down-in-the-heel loafers
crushed beside the dry erase board,
or walking the hallway
to the OK Corral to work ninth graders
at a basketball game
all bright lights and whistles and popcorn.

Armadillos Sought for Leprosy Studies

The armadillo crosses rivers by expelling
the oxygen from its lungs, then sinking,
walks below the surface on the riverbed.
If the river is too wide, often the case,

it drowns, and is eventually swept
to the shallows where it bobs in body gas,
bleaches like a Clorox bottle, the buoy
of a jugline. Armadillos are migrants

with few skills beyond eating insects.
They are neither turtle, nor rabbit.
They leap into the air when scared, spread
their short legs, hiss. They can wander

into a campfire's light and stand confused,
as if transfixed by their pointed noses.
Some are made into handbags, or taxidermic
baskets. At a farm auction, I got into

a bidding war with an old woman over
the only armadillo at the sale. As a teacher,
I used it in my classroom for holding
dry erase markers. Contrary to the chili

cook's joke, they seldom end up in the pot
although 'begrudged as Hoover Hogs' in the 30s.
They are killed by rivers, but mostly by trucks
on state highways. We count their dead

as we drive through Texas. It would become
a game if we weren't sensitive liberals,
woke to the small brain, the leathery shell,
the leprosy of the folks Jesus knew.

Our Dog Wears One Shoe

My wife takes the dog
for a walk. We decide
to use a little shoe
for his injured right paw.
About ten minutes into
the walk, she calls
and says the dog is getting
ready to take a poop.
And I say, that's good.
Then she says that she
forgot to bring
the little plastic bags
to scoop up his mess.
I say, ok.

She says, I was wondering
if you could bring me
a bag. I was right
in the middle of writing
a poem that would
probably change our lives,
but I say, sure. I grab the little
roll of plastic, and drive off
down the street to where
she says she'll be waiting.

I turn the wrong way, north
instead of south, I suppose
still thinking of my poem
lost in suburban beige, and I can't
find them. I see an old man

working in his flower
garden, and I stop to ask
if he's seen an attractive woman
of an indeterminate age
watching a dog with one shoe
taking a dump. He frowns,
thinks I'm speaking in political
metaphors. End of days stuff.

When I find the two of them
standing patiently on the curb,
the dog grins. He sees
my car and starts leaping
up and down like a kid.
Somewhere he lost his shoe.
My wife says, wait a minute,
you can take the bag
home with you. So, I do, and
minutes later, I'm driving
back the way I came
hunting a shoe that fits a dog.

teenagers on the fruit bridge

jumping from the bridge
is like choosing a watermelon
to thump
to plug
to follow the crowd

into
a fruit salad of poor choices
the hospital bed
the morgue
the society for modern eunuchs

the river moves in slow
avocado green
with
coconut husks pineapple spears
gnawed rinds

the boys gauge the current with stones
listening for the whoosh
the depth plunge
the slurp
of spoons in cantaloupes

the girls lean over the pylons
between the river and the sun
lemons & peaches
perfect
strawberries

the boys gasp in admiration
in invitation

in leaping from the bridge
hollering
bananas & plums

Ending Drought

While cleaning out my classroom after
retirement, I found a manilla folder of poems
stuffed between dogeared paperbacks,
poetry scrawled in pencil on notebook paper, yellowed
pages from my first students in my first class.
I was twenty-one when I started teaching,
barely able to manage a Confucius-thin beard.
I just left a commune of hippies. We picked

pears and cut firewood for the future.
I was never sure if I taught eighth graders anything.
On the other hand, I learned about the weather.
When clouds climbed up over the Malt Shop
across from school, the storm demanded
a celebration. The kids turned restless, laughed
and bounced in their wooden desks,
fell in love, became cartoon characters.

I measured behavior with a barometer.
One class swatted flies with their lit books,
opened until a fly settled between the pages,
then they'd snap the cover shut. The flies
died like Emily Dickinson em dashes.
A cordon of boys, just out of gym class,
called me their poetry coach. I needed a whistle
on a lariat. I gave them the rain
as a respite for talking about girls, for stammering
when the high school office aid walked in
wearing her mini skirt and knee-high boots.
There was always football to consider, the next

Thursday night meant more than a grammar lesson.
When I asked them in September to write a short essay
about their summers, several titled their papers SA.
That confused me until I figured out how much
trouble their education was in. One boy,
ran away from home, only
showing up to school for the free lunch.
He turned in his SA without any punctuation.
Baffled, I asked him why he didn't use periods,
commas, question marks. He twisted his neck
towards the door. I don't want
nothin' to end, he said.

Today, with the summer rain building,
I carted the paperbacks to Secondhand Tom's
for ten cents a copy, then I had biscuits
and gravy at Bob's Grill. I kept
the poems to read in my lawn chair,
wondering where they had gone, the fresh faces
that matched the unruly penmanship.
A man stopped at the garage sale next door.
He reminded me of the boy who wrote a haiku
about a Busch Light commercial, nearly
perfect in its 5-7-5 syllable count, it's use
of snow as a season word, his kigo.
I watched him compare the wiggle in two flyswatters,
recognizing the mop of hair, but not
the ZZ Top beard. He turned
his head in my direction and slowly grinned—
Hey Coach, he said, you were my teacher.

American Socialist

April Muscle

A man and a boy and a dog walk
down to the water's edge. The lake

is gray like the sky, the air warm like silk.
Behind the hill across the water is a shelter.

A musician practices runs on a baritone.
The notes carry farther than the shore,

up the small ravines to the pasture, notes
double tongued, some clean,

some sputtered and begun again. The dog
chases a tennis ball into the water.

The boy jumps on his toes at the man's side.
The dog swims with the ball in his mouth,

only the bell of his head above water,
his eyes on the man, his single note.

Transplanting Irises

My daughter and I drove dirt roads
with a shovel and a bucket in the pickup bed,
hunting for asparagus, lilies, cane,
whatever volunteered freely.
We divided a family of irises, long wild,
abandoned along a fence row
on the county's side of the ditch, spread
from where a driveway had been
to where a mailbox had stood.
                    There is history in
dividing a clump of irises, a story
more of intention than of name or date.
One woman's shovel of hope, probably
dug after breakfast was cooked, after
her children had gone off to school,
after her husband had taken the tractor
from the barn to the field. There's no
practical reason to plant irises
when food money is scarce, when
the mortgage payment is due.
                    One truth
we could count on from this most
feminine of flowers was leaving
what we've transplanted for another to find
in purples and blues and whites,
a passing on of what's been passed on
to someone with a shovel
and an empty spot in the sun.

Mice in the Coal Fields

The office car is abandoned
on a spur of railroad track. It is filled
with dust and gray sunlight. Some windows
are locked in their final shutting,
others broken or riveted with .22 caliber holes.
The door hangs on a single hinge, jamb split,
shattered by vandals. The mining company,
long gone under, has stripped the pastures of the coal
that lay soft and bituminous in its belly.
Bills of sale, receipts, orders indecipherable
litter the floor, catch the breeze, flutter like birds.
The miners who made the transition
from deep shaft to strip mining
drew small pensions or moved on to more
promising veins. Mice run the floorboards,
stuffing file cabinets with fescue, bits of letterhead,
mimeographed paperwork. Even in triplicate
commerce is consumed by mildew, by rough
bark dogwood, by switchgrass. The end
of each workday brings more loose shale.
Overhead a turkey buzzard circles, feathers
like piano keys fingered by wind.

In the Flint Hills Near Bazaar, Kansas

Nearby, Knute Rockne's plane crashed.
The site is probably marked with a small sign,
a plaque on a cairn. I don't know.

I'm driving without research, looking
to lose myself in the folds of the hills—green,
treeless, as open as the sky is open. Something

I hope to find is beyond the next rise,
a dry creek bed, an abandoned farmhouse,
a windmill on iron legs. More of what

I'm searching for has to do with time, more
than structure, more than place. It is a sense
of being enfolded, bound by hills, found

by an anonymous wind, feathered
like the hawk is feathered, or a small plane
muted by decades of green prairie.

American Socialist

Funny how the days in a month fly.
It seems like only yesterday that October
shuffled into the room, dragging yellow leaves,
and now, it's stepping out into the dim rust.

It's time for my monthly pension check.
I can pay for the extravagances of the past weeks,
coffee for tomorrow, carry out Chinese, Netflix.
For a few days I'm flush with discovery,

a silver dollar in a box of copper coins.
I keep a roll of fives in my pocket, hand one
to the guy in the parka with the cardboard sign.
He mumbles a blessing. I nod to him, say

take care brother. Then it's just the leaves
in my pants cuffs, the acorns at my feet
cracking, toes like typewriter keys,
like little hammers on the sidewalk.

First Chill

For the first time in weeks, you wear
the Patagonia jacket, tighten
the laces on your leather boots, walk
the trail through the familiar woods.
When it is your time to go, and here,
you are referring to the final departure,
there is a fondness
for things you can touch, the beaten
deer wallow, the tall grass rifled
with thistle and goldenrod.
There is melancholia, of course, gray clouds,
saddle soap on old leather,
the things of a poem. On the other hand,

a hawk, wind in his wings, is gone
behind the ridge the moment
you turn your head. His tracks in the wind
are as invisible as your breath.
The intangible is what you cannot bear to lose,
here, where love drops leaves, where
tomorrow rumbles in the west.
A small boy in a hoodie
keeps step with his grandfather.
Both know the path through the trees.
They speak easily as if time itself
is sheltered by the sky.

Emily Dickinson Died Behind a Hedge

Books of poetry are slim, knife slim,
some for carving wood, others butter.
On occasion volumes as thick as a Bible
thump the market table, lifetime collections
from a great poet, who surrounds her tomb
with blades from across her life. Then too,
there's the eccentric with a few bucks
saved from selling the family car,
financing his best words in hardbound,
maybe with a dust cover (which he'll need),
and with a prayer to Emily Dickinson,
he hand-delivers copies to libraries, then
shelves the rest, moths in a cardboard box,
dedicated in the frontispiece to someone
at an estate sale, who is nearly, but not
                              quite as dead.

Cemetery in Kansas

Where the brown people are buried
the stones have fallen, sometimes
tossed into piles or carted into ravines.
Crows in the hedgerow of their choir.
Farmers plow the fields over the dead,
grow beans and alfalfa, corn for the cattle
they graze between the mounds
of slowly sinking earth. In December
no place is colder than an open field,
the black angus bunched against the wall
of a barn, a shed stuffed with hay.
All that remains of the lives turned under
is a plaintive wind, the raking cold.

Old Guy with a Pencil

writes too many poems,
imagines people poised
over cups of coffee, waiting
to read his next line. Autumn

leaves litter his yard. They drop
like nothing in November matters
but the falling. He has not
combed his hair since his wedding.

He worries that he's become
the old guy with too many anecdotes,
the one avoided at party's
or in the grocery check-out line.

He taps his pencil on his desk,
remembers the woodpecker
invisible in the woods, often
the only sound before snow.

Graduation Photo 1949

I know the town, this grade school
where the 6th grade class poses in three lines,
a teacher and the principal on each wing.
One boy wears a sport's jacket, his top
shirt button fastened at his throat.
He stands next to the teacher, a pet maybe.
No one smiles, although a couple of the boys
seated cross-legged in the front row, sport
the edge of a smirk, their lips turned up,
and held secretly for the camera. Mostly,
I'm taken by the poverty in their eyes,
like a row of closed windows.
I know enough of this town to recognize
the neighborhood, home to disheveled
hand-me-downs, thin socks on skinny ankles.
Some of the girls have ribbons in their hair.
It is a brave show. Not a single student looks
beyond the camera at the playground
they're soon to leave. Next year they will
walk the extra blocks to the junior high,
across Broadway and down the hill
on Adams Street. Their shoes will shine
from the morning dew, ragged short-cuts
across the railroad tracks,
past the large homes, garden lawns, birdbaths
splashed with birds they don't recognize.

In Santa Fe with New Family

We've been visiting Spanish missions
all morning. Each one has a story about
long suffering. My stepson and I
are standing at the foot of an altar,
looking up at a particularly graphic crucifix.
My stepson says, who is that guy?
And I think, O Jesus wife,
What have you taught this boy?

She later explains she was raised a Methodist
in a church with a beautiful pipe organ.
The choir recorded an album of Christmas songs.
She learned to paddle a canoe at summer camp,
kissed her first boy on a church trip to Six Flags.
For bleeding, her MYF counselor explained,
we have Band-Aids, methylate, and tampons.

Intervention

The family dog has a rabbit trapped
under the deck, or maybe it is better
to say, the rabbit has the dog trapped,
tethered to the pressure treated wood.
He orbits, single-minded like a storm
on a chain, swinging from stanchion
to stanchion. We've seen the rabbit
only as a silhouette, unhurried
in the shadows. The dog squeezes
his shoulders into the darkness.
I pull him out by his hindlegs, fill in
the hole, cover it with chicken wire.
This is no way to live, an addict.
You should see yourself in a mirror.

Euclid's Dog

This middle school kid at the dog park is full of himself.
He laughs at my dog because his anus
is shaped like a triangle. I'd never thought

of my dog geometrically before, but the boy is right,
his coat is trimmed in a perfect isosceles.
I felt the boy's laughter embarrassing to my dog.
As a former teacher he was just the kind of kid

who made my classroom Napoleonic, a Waterloo.
I tell him to keep watching. My dog poops little pyramids.
If four of them are stacked together,
they make a perfect cube, harmonic,

a Euclidean puzzle. The boy starts to smile
but stops, holds the cube in his brain like a poop bag.
He trots across the park
and knocks the ballcap off his brother's head.

In the Parking Lot

The young man, a former student,
said he was tired of waiting, and was
ready to join the stats of the pandemic.
I winced behind my mask, forty years
his senior, but in good health. So,
he went on, I live the way I want
until it catches me, or until it doesn't.
There's too much blue sky to shelter
under a cloud. I get it. Possibly once,
I would have danced the same dance.
Today is different. I work part time
at an antique mall, the elderly walk
the aisles, reminiscing, pointing out
the past, the price tags, what mother
or grandmother used on the farm.
They cling to remembering like
frail cranes, behind masks, under
the grey rain which is the horizon.

The High School Class Graduates

without masks tonight. For some,
it is an unveiling, boys with new beards,
girls with touches of blush & lip sheer.
They are no longer children, flippant
with smartphones & Instagram.
Most understand the lyrics of the songs
they sing. Because of the pandemic,
they graduate under the lights
on the football field, folding chairs
between the hashmarks. Tonight,
they worry their names will be mis-
pronounced over the loudspeakers,
vowels falling off a stranger's tongue,
consonants sputtered like quarter notes.
The girls pin back their hair & slip-on
difficult heels. The boys swagger
like they imagine they must.

First Bell

They look to you from behind
cotton masks, to call them Kilroy
would be as foreign as an allusion
to Mr. Bill, to rotary phones,
hybrid schedules, plexiglass carrels.
Many are concerned
about fall sports, cheerleaders
without a team to shish ka boom.
Some play it cool, flat-lined, as blank
as tablet paper. By next period,
they will be vaping in the toilet stall.
But every eye is on you, young teacher.
You are their intermediary between
planets, their swift Greek. Upper classmen
feign indifference. It is their schtick.
All listen when you ask, what is next,
pop quizzes, Socratic seminars,
journals, poetry slams?
When the bell rings, they wonder
do we crack the spines on
algebra books, take notes on the fall
of ancient civilizations? Rome
burned a million years ago. The skies
are orange with fire. Black men,
like neo-Christians,
cry out in the streets. Pro football
is back. Politicians toss Covid stats
like Hail Marys, like scarecrows
across sweet corn. Nothing ripens. Nothing
is left to pick from the stalk.
You know they need words, a language

to put a face to the times. But all
you can think of is Charles Bukowski
at the post office, Lorca in Spain,
the missing body of Lew Welch,
Gary Snyder finding his suicide note,
then fighting fires in the Sierras.
The Jesus girl waits on the rapture.
The Goth chick wants more Buddha.
Bill wants better pot, Jordy
the stats for the Chief's game.
They test the profane on you, making light
with what is dark, what teenagers do
when powerless and confused.

The Dog Slobbers on My Wife's
Down Booties

Her booties stink of dog spit.
So, she runs them through
the gentle cycle on the Kenmore.
I toss them in the dryer
with a couple of chewed towels.
When she returns from her walk
with Stanley, the house
smells like an overcooked duck.
The boots have exploded,
the dryer filled with feathers,
dandelion tufts, white plumules.
Stanley is thrilled, his nose soon
matted with bird. He is banned
to the backyard. We try to sweep
feathers into a dustpan,
but it is hopeless, down fluffs
lift into flight with each gust
of the broom, circle
the linoleum, migrating
to the carpet, the bedroom,
the organized sky just south
of the bi-fold doors.

After Cutting the Grass

I dump a fist of ice cubes in my water glass,
leave three on the floor for the dog.
For a moment, all that I have missed today
is this cold water, the dog crunching ice
at my feet. But nothing lasts,
and soon I am standing at the door,
waiting for the sun to move,
for the rain that is two days away.
Earlier, I ordered flowers for a funeral.
I tried to imagine a light poem
to make my sister laugh, her family
walking into the funeral home
in their throwaway masks, sitting
together in the air conditioning, and there
would be my flowers, fresh from the florist,
the same old words, the same old death,
swelling in the heat like a cicada.

Building a Bridge

I am not an architect, nor
do I understand the mathematics
of relationships. For instance,
those supported by only one truss,
wife or husband. One solid, stanchioned
to gravity, the other spinning
out into space, man or woman,
above a canyon or a river
or a city of sparkling lights.
In architecture, measurements
are exact, like ratios to a ballpark's
upper deck, or to a sunroom's acrobatics,
extending dizzily over a cliff.
But these equations make me
as giddy as the view.
Between a wife and a husband,
I think the beams, when cantilevered,
one flying, always outward,
must be interchangeable, or else,
through lack of tensile strength,
crack, and, as in a failed metaphor,
the other will fly too far for suspension
to bear. A good bridge, on the other hand,
with two beams extending, let's say,
over the Royal Gorge or the Golden Gate
or the Hudson River, meet somewhere
in midair. Crazy as it sounds, two spans,
coming from opposite directions,
joined by nuts and bolts,
become the steel in the other's strength.

The Farmer's Market

I walk the isles with only
one intention, homegrown
tomatoes. The vendors
have tables full, over-
flowing with vegetables,
jars of honey, Kansas fruit--
peaches, blackberries.
A truck on the street sells
Kansas City hot dogs, buried
under onions, chili, and
pickled relish. Everyone I
see is masked-up, bottles
of hand sanitizer beside
cash boxes. Paper towels.
I walk the dog. He pulls
at the leash, sniffs his way
past the No Pets Allowed
sign. No touching
the produce. Exact cash only.
I turn the dog in a circle
as we head back towards
the entrance. I point towards
a basket of red tomatoes,
another jalapenos. The
dog is a problem. He prefers
frog legs, squirrel. The vendor
laughs, muffled behind cotton.
She hurries our order
before security (if they have
one among city farmers)
beats us with a fresh zucchini.

Another Monday

My wife clips my hair this morning,
just the sideburns, the little wings
that flare at the sides, unruly,
devoid of product. She evens
it all with a comb,

the snip snip of the thousand
nights smoothed together.
Soon, I will be presentable,
a worthy estimation of myself.

She finds a hole in my new shirt,
lifts it into the light beside the Maytag.
There are ways to fix this. I think
of birds flying through the morning,
lacing together the gaps left by clouds,
by the moon, by the fallen stars,
sewing the edges of the sky together.

planting a daffodil
for someone
I will never know

Eating Tater Tots
at the Jingo Diner

Hunting Pocket Watches Before the Election

The pawn shop is busy this afternoon,
the gun counter elbowed up with shoppers.
It's like a third world Black Friday. A clerk
explains to one old man that his background check
could take 15 minutes or 15 days depending.
The glass counter that used to hold silver coins
and failed marriage jewelry has been converted
to pistols and boot knives. There is
not a time piece in the shop, beer signs have been
replaced with taxidermy mounts. There's still
a shelf of power tools, nail guns mostly.
I try on a gas mask, check my profile
in the convex mirror. With my Covid haircut
I look a bit like Attila the Hun's second cousin,
Bernie, the one who pillaged the Roman bath
for monogramed towels and travel shampoos.

Cledith's Farm

I saw this painting at an auction,
an oil on canvas, signed with an obscure
swirl in the bottom right corner.

It is of a country road, curving downhill
into a small town. The road is dirt,
the trees bend over it like village elders,

shading a few houses, a general store
with a gas pump, a long front porch
with an awning, a public telephone.

The colors have dulled, which is not
surprising, considering the foxed canvas,
the antique stretchers, probably

pulled out of a closet or a barn,
at best, the bedroom of a farmhouse,
the room used by guests, relatives
like the nephew home from the Army.

Before shipping out, he wakes early
and needs to sit on the edge of the mattress
before facing the breakfast table.

The painting will sell for a few bucks.
It will look best hanging at a distance
from across a room, like history itself
when painted with color gone quiet.

Dirty Laundry

Tired of airing his laundry, the novelist
decides to write in the third person,
focusing on tradesmen in a small village
in late medieval England.
His main character is a cooper,
known for his cured oaken casks.
The village is south of London,
a coastal town, a day's cart ride from Weymouth.
Gulls pester the barrel maker at an inn table.
He shoos them with one hand while he spoons
his pottage with the other. The innkeeper's
daughter fills his cup from a pitcher.
She wears a blue ribbon in her auburn hair.
Her eyes are green with promise. Her mother,
a pocked, petulant woman, snaps a bedsheet
from an upper window. Fishwives
ignore the rat, escaping down
the mooring line from a French boat.
Always the rat, the fleas, the innkeeper's mouser
dozing on an empty barrel.

In the Snow with Two Million Refugees

The dog and I wander out
between the houses to the dogwood
                to piss out the day
without the neighbor lady spying,
without the police at my door.
I imagine explaining my business
                to them, time
to weigh the two million, to breathe
the end of the day, to wonder,
as the moon edged the clouds,
how old the night is,
how familiar
the moon and the cold are together.

It is easy to forget we are fragile
without skullcaps, without sweaters,
without television to tell the stories
                that warm us.

In the snow I etch a design
like a boy will. It is a boat, medieval,
with a refugee's prow, and by
                the single mast

the dribble of all we can save.

Russians Dig Trenches in the Red Forest

Opening the kitchen door
to let the dog out tonight,
he pauses, and I think it's the rain
still dripping from the eaves

from the everything left out
before the clouds settled,
but then I realize he's listening,
to a new sound—
first frogs along the tree line, swelling
into the living pines, the mulch

of old songs
reminding us of the garden hoe,
wild asparagus, new lettuce,
surprisingly forgotten
after months of freeze,
after months of blankets,
gas logs, television,
noses buried in CNN

before war irradiated the news,
before Russian shovels
turned graves, dug
poison trenches instead of turnips.

Not All Russians Are Assholes

The mailbox is frozen shut. The mailman
smacks the ice away with his fist, drives
down the road towards the next box
planted on a fence post, leaning from years
of constant wind. They are stuffed with
brochures, catalogued
cruises down European rivers, a time-share
on Marco Island, a glossy envelope of hybrid
tomato seeds for the tray in the window.

There hasn't been a real letter to open
since Wi-Fi reached the plains, since Google
ran its highspeed cable next to the barbed wire.
In the church office, the minister
searches conspiracy theories for simple answers
to complex problems. Blades
of winter wheat green-up through the sleet
of today's storm. In years past,
homesteaders planted Russian seeds
that could survive Kansas winters
when nothing grew
except the hope of meadowlarks.

Eating Tater Tots at the Jingo Diner

My neighbor has been
eating poorly cooked bats.
Now, he has Covid. I've
been lecturing him all month
to cook them thoroughly.
Buy bleach.
Well-done is the only way
to prepare a winged mammal.
They are creatures of the night,
of mysterious sonar, and
of darting flight. They poop
huge piles of crap which
can be used for saltpeter
in primitive gunpowder.
The Chinese of Wuhan
taught us that much. Bats
are not Christian. They obey
a foreign call. Trump
has been right all along.
There's no need for masks, or
the hoodoo of science.
Facts f**k with really true truth.
It's better to raise up
a colorful urban legend
and wear it on your sleeve
with authority. I choose bats,
because they are creepy,
exotic in a food stall, and
easy to skewer.

Vaccination

If I could be born again,
and I don't mean at a tent revival,
but from another mother
at another time. I'd choose
to be taller. Being the shortest
kid in grade school, a kid
with a funny nickname,
notched a chip on my shoulder, made me

pugnacious, short-sighted.
In junior high the boys grew like wheat,
but I stayed short, skinny,
with the world view of a green onion.
I did my best to change my name.
My father bought me a fake gold ID bracelet
with two letters inscribed on its oval tag,
a short name, a pawn shop sobriquet.
I planned to give the bracelet to Kim or Kristie or Kathy,
but I feared school mixers,
especially slow dances, my partner gazing
across the top of my skull.

If from her perspective, she could
see into my brain
she wouldn't find lurid sexual fantasies,
but dreams of elevator shoes.
Somehow, this all reminds me of the vaccination
we will soon be ticketed to take,
a queue of souls in plastic chairs,
hoping to drop the masks, the bone rattle,
rolling up shirtsleeves, sucking in

the medicinal swab.
In my case, I'll watch the needle
to the point of the stick,
smallpox, polio, shingles, Covid-19,
whatever the name.

In terms of rebirth, well, forget it.
I am tall enough to slow dance
alone in the mirror.

The Supreme Court Cocks the 2nd Amendment

Yesterday, the foot trail we walked was a tunnel,
a rabbit run through currant and sumac. Today, a jungle.

We found Queen Anne's Lace and Poison Hemlock
(easily confused), the first a hairy stem, the other

smooth with spots of purple like an old person's skin,
the hands, the arms, wattles to the chin.

One is edible, a wild carrot with a tap root
fit for a lunchroom. The other killed Socrates, ends

us all in a salad, a cup of tea. Identification
is tricky. They both rise from disturbed ground

like a just cause, like a calling. White flowers
are lace to morning's trigger. The hungry hour.

Understanding is in the stem, the backbone
that holds the bloom, keeps (they say) the table safe,

the school a home away from home.

The Demagogue of Fat

First, there must be an emptiness, a hollow
at the base of the throat, the stomach, the heart.
Often, there is a yammering in the ears,
a clamor of clanking pans and rattling rakes.
Amid the noise, a brass gong, louder
than the rest, beats with a resonance that fills
the concave stomach, the empty breast.
The brain, starved of oxygen, blues
like old cauliflower. There is little thinking,
only colors, images of discord. Second,
there must be a dissonance between neighbors,
a finger to point, a fist to shake at a goat.
Finally, a loudmouth to wag the dog,
to promise what has been lost,
to shake the canine bones until its jaws snap.

Lunch at the Refugee Cafe

This cafe serves whoever has escaped
by boat, through tunnels, over walls; has
been sliced by wire, shrapnel, coyoted
across deserts, through rain forests, over snowcaps.
All that can be salvaged stuffed
in Captain America backpacks, wrapped
in Chicago Bulls t-shirts, zip locked
against inclemency.

New recipes are spiced with paprika,
turmeric, ghost pepper. Every ingredient,
every man, woman, child,
is from somewhere else,
if not now, then once, when a mother,
a grandmother, a great grandmother
packed a bag, stepped into the cloud
of unknowing. Only Native Americans
have a claim to pre-history.

At today's cafe, there is a sneeze guard.
Clean plates. Stainless forks. Spoons concave
with soup. With reflection.

Knives are for butter.
Masks have been worn for centuries.

Reading William Stafford After the Russians
Shell the Nuclear Reactor at Zaporizhzhia

There's a place in the woods where we walk,
dog ahead, nosing out voles, the scent of rabbits,
whatever has left itself behind from the night.

I follow, slower than I once did, but still
able with my one good eye to see
that the trees are junipers, blue berries lit
with tomorrow, more vivid than the evergreen's

fan of needles, the spray of stored sunlight.
In the deep branches an invisible bird
breaks into trills, songs to warn others of our passing.
We have our moment here today,

and tomorrow, well maybe, we are just a trail,
what we've left behind from our daylight,
boot prints in the mud, paw prints circling
back upon themselves, a good nose, an eye

on hope, following a trail through the woods
without war, without bombs, without fires
which tomorrow's children must fight.

Covid Baseball at Kauffman Stadium

Do you remember the movie
with Bernie Lomax, the dead guy
with the ritzy beach house in the Hamptons?
He's in the stands this week, although
he slumps a bit, sunglasses cocked,
nonplussed as a resin bag. A cardboard
Patrick Mahomes is nearby,

his 2020 smile
on a glossy cutout. Living
pitchers struggle for a toehold on the rubber.
Canned stadium noise is piped in
with the organ. Fans in front of televisions
imagine themselves easy
among the cardboard celebrities, cornering
foul balls behind empty seats.

Searching for a Comet with Binoculars

You train your glasses midway
between the Big Dipper
and the tree-lined horizon.
There is a smudge of light
where the comet should be, as close
to the earth, as near to
today, as it ever will appear,
its thousand-mile tail stretched
into the past, ice and dust
reflecting sun. On the lake dock
you plant your feet, turning the focus
wheel to the right, to the left.
Four ducks streak the starlight.
They are creases, folding
and unfolding in your brain.
The whippoorwill begins
to wail, all you have
in understanding comets is a hunch,
like with insight, like with faith,
the binocular dial a little
this way, a little that.

Utopian Gravy

Learning Knots

As an Eagle Scout, he wished
he'd earned a merit badge
about Girls, if one existed

he imagined a fully embroidered
cheerleader backed with Velcro,

.

a patch his mother wouldn't have
to sew onto his sash.

Penis Envy

I was jealous of Robert's
ability to dribble a basketball.
As a point guard he knew
all the moves, behind his back,
between his legs.

The Men's Club

The door to the men's room
is locked, only those
who are already inside
can get out. It takes
a special key to use
the special toilet paper.
I shit you not.

Advent Calendar

First, rain, then ice crystals
pelt the cat on the steps
to your house. If you
are his Jesus, you should
open the door and let him in.

Thursday Night

I can only imagine
what you were thinking

at the Last Supper with
the olives, unleavened bread,
lamb chops, the wine
that was blood

and someone ordering
the Caesar salad.

Second Childhood

There's a place in my jaw
where I used to have a
tooth, my tongue

searches it like a vacant lot
for lost baseballs.

A Game with a Ball

Tonight, the moon reaches its zenith behind clouds. Snow
builds on snow. The dog and I slip out of the house into the
bitter piss-time before sleep. He sniffs the edge of the night,
the blade of time passing. I am doing the same, head raised
from my jersey, from the chili powder, the onion, the garlic
of a half-time potluck.

We are in mourning over the Super Bowl, a game with a ball.
My granddaughter cries for Patrick Mahomes, his Kansas
City magic, tonight so fragile, an ice crystal on the tongue.
I explain to her, as my father did to me in 1960, after Bill
Mazeroski nailed the Yankees in the 9th, that seasons follow
seasons. Even in a pandemic, tomorrow wins.

It is near zero without windchill. In minutes my toes are ice.
I zip my vest, wait for the dog to finish his single job. We
listen for the first sound to startle the tree limbs, to crack the
ceiling of the sky. A rabbit appears in the moonlight between
the hedge and the fence. The dog thumps across the snow.
At times, all four clumsy paws are airborne, athletic, caught in
a light which is neither gentle nor cruel.

Utopian Gravy

I take Stanley to the dog park. He smiles and runs with the other dogs, swims, splashes through shallows on the long path through the woods. Constantly, he turns and looks back to see if I'm in sight, trailing like a compass. I look forward to snowstorms. We walk through the wind whipped flakes. Find our way into the quiet trees like early Americans with the west stretched out ahead. There was a hope then that the past could be left behind, that discovery awaited the next turn in the river or rise to a tree-lined horizon. Vegetarians could create their own town, build a palisade, eat all the eggplant they could swallow. Even the shakers found a way to live, until they died off, until all the future held was a few sticks of very plain furniture. Maybe they complained. Maybe they regretted the long wait for heaven. Maybe they didn't know what they were signing up for and were as horny as monks until the end.

Onion bulbs
swell in today's stew, your tears
on the knife blade

If I lived in the 19th century and was inclined to start my own community, I'd dedicate it to chicken fried steak and gravy-loaded mash potatoes. We'd live happily ignorant without cholesterol checks until we choked-up the fuel lines. And then we'd have our own graveyard with extra-large coffins, and after each funeral, we'd be carried in sturdy little goat carts to a farewell supper in the community center.

spooning too much
    sugar into my coffee,
    the bitter wind

Lucid Beavers

I.

One morning Chester woke up from a pretty satisfying
sleep. It had rained during the night. He loved the sound
of rain and thunder and wind lifting the branches outside
his window. So, when he opened his eyes that morning, he
decided that waking wasn't good enough for him. Sleep, or
rather, the pleasant dreams he had while drifting in and out
of sleep were better. He closed his eyes and dreamed up a
cabin in the woods, probably in the mountains. But then he
decided that a cabin would take too long to build. Even in
a dream, he was practical. So, he made it a trailer. Probably
an Airstream, since he'd always been enamored by them,
especially how they curved the world like a convex mirror. He
switched the mountainside to a forest, one with oak trees and
a running stream. The running stream was important because
he thought it would be soothing to watch the stream rise
and fall over the months ahead. The oak trees he wasn't so
sure about. In time they'd be pinging acorns onto his trailer
and keeping him awake when he was in his dream sleep in
his dream Airstream. Walnut trees were worse. Maples might
work except for those crazy little helicopter seeds.

II.

Yes, he decided. Seeds of all kinds were the problem. And
they created a momentary dilemma for his dreamworld. The
only answer was not to think of them. Every time a seed
popped, he'd send it away. Didn't matter what kind. Float
them like a canoe down the stream that rose and fell beside
the Airstream. He thought he could handle that until he
noticed one morning that the creek was so full of canoes,

rafts, pirogues, johnboats, that he had to create a small River Patrol, complete with dark green uniforms and black leather belts. They cleaned out the backlog of seed- craft with an airboat, and in their zeal, swept away the beginning of a beaver dam.

III.

The beavers must have snuck in during the night while Chester had drifted into a non-rem state. Otherwise, he would have noticed and made up some rules for them to follow. Beavers need to be clear on these things. Otherwise, they create their own boundaries. At first, the beavers were unhappy. Many of them mumbled among themselves behind Chester's back. But they didn't have a lot of options since it was Chester's dream. Chester agreed to let them stay if they kept to their side of the creek. Frankly, he enjoyed watching them, chipping away at trees, swimming with their dog-like heads just cresting the water. It was nearly a perfect set-up. Until the River Patrol captain, an Italian with black greasy hair, told Chester that he'd have to move his Airstream because he was too close to a woodland species, aka the beavers, who preferred privacy. Fuck this, Chester said to the River Patrol captain. Who do you think you're talking to? The captain looked hurt. He said he was just enforcing the laws of a free-flowing eco-system. The beavers watched from the opposite bank as unflappable as ceramic Buddhas. No one was budging.

squeeze

Lodestone

If you think you can measure
a parent's love, show me first the instrument

of measurement, not an altimeter,
or a barometer, or a pressure gauge,
not a jeweler's scale, or some astronomer's

parallax trigonometry. It is not
measured in Celsius or Fahrenheit,
decibels or wave amplitude.

Maybe a compass will do, I'll give you that,
the directional arrow, painted red and black, turns
to the magnetic pole, no matter how the compass
spins on the map, the map spread on a table,

or laid across the dash of a car, or folded,
held horizontal by the hiker's level guess.
Even as the earth curves, wobbles
on an invisible axis, this hemisphere's north

is true like a pelican to a lake
or a moth to a lightbulb.

First Photographs

The twins arrived early this morning.
Of course, they're beautiful, red-faced

and puckered from labor. The parents,
new at this baby business, smile in all

the photographs. The mother tired, worn
from the past nine months, the last

twelve hours. The father,
broad-beamed like a boat, uncertain

of the role he's assumed. Behind
the camera, both grandmothers snap

photographs before the moment
slips into a photo album, before these

swaddled bundles unwrap themselves
and demand only selfies.

No No Know

The grandbaby is coming over today.
For the next eight hours, my wife
and I will take turns holding him
on the couch, tilting his formula bottle
into his mouth, patting his back
for the burp he can't manage. Today
is all one Yes. It is understood in
attention to bottle warmth, a sleep sack,
a monitor clenched to the crib.
Baby proofing the house will come later
after he's turned over, struggled
to his hands and knees, crawled
across the floor towards electrical outlets,
the cabinet below the sink. Wherever
there is danger, he will hear the word No
banging across his life
like a drum, a claxon, an electric fence.
No will require repetition, a firm
presence of adult mind. It will take time,
probably the rest of his life to accept,
stopping him from a fall,
from touching the stove, from tasting
pills in the medicine bottle. He will
learn No as a reminder that bones
can break, that breathing is temporary,
that sometimes hurt cannot be fixed,
and that no is to know.

A Man on a Fast Horse

My father-in-law kept a workshop
next to his garage. After retiring
from pattern making, his quality tools
stood on the oil-soaked floor like

sleeping horses, each had a name,
or in this case, a use. All of which
were obscure to me, an English teacher
who seldom nailed two boards together.

My wife loved her father's shop,
her childhood spent in the doorway,
inhaling the wood dust, the machine oil,
watching her father curry

impossible life into dead
lumber. He had an eye for precise
measurement, knew how to make a cut
with a sharp blade. He used to joke

that a man on a fast horse at fifty feet
wouldn't know the difference
if his cuts were true, or if the glue
gluing two halves of a plank

appeared invisible.

Storm Damage

It is almost as if the earth is a tomato today,
unblemished by pandemic, by the cut worm
that chews the internet, that feeds on the polemics
of cult and party. Carpenters,
a house over, hammer particle board sheeting
onto old trusses. They have been busy
since dawn, ripping away the storm-damage,
shoveling shingles from the roof into dumpsters.
They start early to take advantage of the morning,
before the sky darkens, before the rain.
No one asks to see green cards or papers.
They speak the language of hammers and nails.
Traffic on 87th Street, only a block distant,
hums like any Tuesday in a busy city.
There is business to be done. The Cajun
food truck opens its window, raises
an awning into the hardware store
parking lot. They specialize in alligator
on a stick, shrimp on dirty rice,
deep fried chicken strips. Commerce, for better
or worse, is the voice of blue jays and crows,
the nuthatch in the Rose of Sharon,
the goldfinch zigzagging between shadows.
We are unafraid of work, sweeping
sidewalks, pruning dead limbs,
placing the nail that secures the moon.

Cutting My Covid Ponytail

I think I need a change. Possibly,
it is as simple as cleaning out my desk,
maybe cutting my hair
back to its conservative, pre-pandemic wave.
Maybe it's time to "bite through" the old
as the I Ching says and move on.
Take, for instance, the story
of the photographer in Yellowstone
who refused to give space to the grizzly bear
and her two cubs, for want of a picture, it is said
she held her ground,
which in some ways is notable
like dedication and courage are notable, but then
there's the bear to consider,
and the bear's euthanasia if she'd managed to bite
through the photographer's lens,
a Hugh Glass maiming, a death.

Bears do not survive such attacks.
They are not relocated to some high mountain
and a return to huckleberries.
And the cubs, well, orphaned, they'd be brought
into government care, a cage, a high-fenced compound,
or maybe, too, sent to join their mother.
I do not know how biting-through works entirely.
There are moments in life, mine for sure,
probably yours, when we stand our ground,
gassed by adrenaline or hubris or great denial,
and like the photographer, we bite through
our dull routine, and like a photographer
take the shot, snap the shutter.

Again, I don't know for sure. As a boy,
I rode on the top of a car, a Dodge Dart floored to 70,
arms stretched, fingers clenched on the roof gutters,
seldom more alive, or stupid, than in the windy moonlight.
It was a game we played on Saturday nights.
A country game better than football.
In some ways, less dangerous than romance,
less dangerous than a lot that needs bitten, chewed, swallowed.
Even now, as a I consider a post Covid haircut,
I regret little about country roads.
Sometimes when I'm out on the lawn
as the house sleeps
with the garden manicured
and flowered in peony beds, I long
for something to bite through,
something to end, something to begin.

After Her Husband's Stroke, Linda Ties a Bell to the Dog's Collar

She listens as her dog moves without her towards the creek,
worrying he won't return when she calls, the slope

steep to the water, the brush
as thick as a beard, the silence deep. There is consolation
in listening to the bell, almost as if seeing
the paths he follows down rabbit runs and doe trails.
Even though the dog cannot speak,
he returns with stories tagged to his coat, ticks and burrs
    and briars.
She has heard them all—

the rabbits he chased, the voles that disappeared.

squeeze

the first robin before sunrise
is too full
    of himself to eat, he perches
on a branch of pin oak, warbles
in a dark hood beyond
        the kitchen window

then the crow, invisible
in lake fog, caws
like he has all winter,
    no stranger to our nonfiction,
        to our darker stories,
        to our Hitchcock dreams

    then the woodpecker
drums the hollow tree
that hides larva,
the budding thorn,
    tomorrow's mayapple
rooted deeper than freeze

sparrows at the feeder

soon geese honk up the lake channel,
they sound confused, fly circles
above yesterday's ice, once
        thawed, then
frozen, again thawed, again
        and again

    this morning

I forget myself,
      this skin that wraps
            my bones, sets its ivory
            out on the curb
            with the cans and bottles

recycle
      the partly penciled
     crossword puzzle

Warbler Promise

If each species had one brain
(warblers a brain, starlings a brain),
shared like the sky is shared,
I'd better understand bird flight,
and how they rise, fall, turn
as if on signal.
In spiraling
the flock is a cloud,
only faster than a cloud,
wing variations muted by distance.
In murmuration, they speak
to the branches they've left

reaching, reaching
as if to follow, or reaching
as if with open arms, open
to say they wait,
wait like men and women
wait, having vowed
as if with single mind to keep
promises simple, promises
to wait with one brain, one
wing beat together.

Wild Geese

I cannot help but follow a flight of geese,
especially, when they're just above the treetops,
pumping their wings, forming their characteristic V.
Who doesn't look up at this moment? I suppose
only those of us who are completely distracted,
absorbed by purpose, demands—a number cruncher
with a shirt and tie, wrangling keys from his
pocket, an overbearing boss, his weight
bearing down on his shoulders. Once, when I was
in New York, a man passed me on the sidewalk.
He had a cat sitting on his head. The cat, a weight,
was his Village stich. They walked with practiced
ease, a man with a fur turban, a cat with a view.
When geese flew up the river, the man turned
at the waist, the cat rotating with his head.
Geese flew where geese fly. That was that.

Easy Picking

Between the houses
one loud songbird
echoes against the pastel
bat and board siding,
all beige, scrubbable satin.
The green slope where a creek
once ran, is now billeted
below in a culvert, runoff
washing under lawns,
through iron grates
down to the spillway
to Mill Creek. The neighborhood
backs up to the woods, the stone
caprock, the original game trail,
now asphalted, accessible
as a cheeseburger, a Diet Coke.
Deer, fox, bobcat,
follow the creek
from the Kansas River
to the easy picking
on Thursday trash day,
bowls of dog food, rabbits
in shrubs, chicken bones.
The vulture, light
on the wind, bends
the afternoon
with the tip of a wing.

Uprooting the Lilac

Today, we plant a Limelight hydrangea
in the hole where we dug out the lilac,
where just a month ago, I chopped back
the roots with my garage sale axe.
My wife gave up on it ever flowering,
tall and spindly, spreading
everywhere and nowhere at once.
She gave it seven years to get itself together,
to become a lilac goddammit.
The shovel popped and bent as I pried
the root ball from the earth, the brown
soil, greasy with clay, with shards
of sandstone. The tap root gripped
until it gave, and only the silence held.

Redbud Storm

This spring's first storm sets the redbud blossom.
Many brief winters will follow, wet with rain,
snow, licking wind. The country names are metaphors,
dogwood storm, blackberry storm. Cold ensures

the buds, the insurgence of flowers. Anyone
who has shivered, felt the wind seeping under doors,
around windows, knows the sense of dismay,
the lost dog of summer, wandering small, sniffing

out the bulbs of wild onions. Mostly, there is mud,
frozen and refrozen, winter-slick, crystalized.
Anyone who has shivered knows to shelter, to layer
winter coats like blankets, like memories.

Last year spring brought storm with pandemic.
This year war. Blood freezes. We wait.

Mountain Goats on a Highway
West of Aspen

I remember watching for mountain goats
on a steep ridge in Colorado, our small Toyota
flying down the highway towards the interstate.

Probably, I should have pulled off at the Historic
Interest marker, sign bolted to a post, between
the river and the road. The goats, sure-footed,

as easy on the mountain side as sage brush,
remained hidden, stoic as stones, as invisible
as spies. If we'd stopped the car, and stood

beside the roadside marker, it might have read
something about the old stagecoach trail
carved westward out of Aspen, the one

that emptied into Montrose, before beginning
the climb to Ouray, then into the San Juans.
There is no loneliness like an empty road,

especially in cold rain and shushing sage.
Nothing is written about the mountain goats,
then or now, they blend so completely

into the brush, into the granite knuckles.

Red Cup

Up early taking care of dogs.
Hummingbirds halo the feeder. Nurse
coffee among the oak's shade, sweetened
in a red cup. Woodpeckers,
unseen, drum the hardwood
for beetle larvae. The heron leaves
his shadow behind in the mud
and flaps his impossible wings along
the breast of the hillside, milk
doled into warm coffee, the lip
of the cup raised. The gap of
the curtain at the kitchen window
is spread to tomatoes, an onion,
Mexican avocados in a glass bowl.

Rain in the Time of Pandemic

My wife plays with the dog in the kitchen.
Her voice, light, airy, chirps while

he runs circles through the house, fat
puppy feet pounding the hardwood floor.

She laughs like a schoolgirl when he
falls against the cabinets, spilled out like a box

of leather shoes. Upstairs, I sit at my desk
beside the open window, writing

a poem about the rain, a poem of sounds
that I have written before, but

in different words. The dog chews
his squeaky toy, drums the kitchen chairs

with his fetching. The old wind lifts
the leaves to silver against the darkening sky.

Nearing Sedalia

There's a silo along the highway
with a tree growing out of it, the top
branches splayed across the sky
like an umbrella, like an anemone.

It's a landmark for us as we drive
across Missouri, as much a mile marker
as a small town, a fishing creek
with an iron bridge, a cemetery

in a children's game.

We watch for it on the hill
behind the barn, behind the ghost sign
faded across the barn roof for
hickory baskets, walnut bowls, moccasins.

The silo is made from tile bricks,
carefully cemented, the domed roof
of sheet metal and wood collapsed,
blown into the pasture, the sapling

in a brief cylinder of sun.

Acorns on All Saints Day

You walk through the woods,
shuffling leaves like fallen days.

You see more through the trees
than you have since early spring,
the rise of hill, the spur of limestone,
squirrels nesting in high oaks.

Game trails reveal themselves
winding between branches, briar,
and windfall. There's a home
for you in change, feathers

between trees, acorns
dropping like rain. A longing for
all you've loved reaches beyond
your farthest step, almost further

than hope, the moving sap,
the flowing heartwood.

Feathered Iron

Some mornings in November
just when you think the last
warm days are behind you, the sun
rises warmer than usual over the rooftops
and the wren, you've listened to
all summer, reappears from somewhere
and belts out a few notes. It's
surprising because you've thought
the bird in flight, made an entry of it
in your daily journal. But here she is
singing like its late summer again.
So where does she go with her
wren house vacant, returning
like a loud memory. The morning
is crisp, frost
feathering the iron patio furniture.
So, why does she bother, the only
bird left from summer. Surely,
there's more hope in flight
than in staying put, waiting for
what she knows is coming.

Dog, We Are One Stop from the Trailer Park

down by the river a good guess,
we will own nothing but an old broom,
and a five-gallon bucket for cans.

My wife starts the vacuum
to pick up the slivers of ostrich bone
that the dog has chewed.
She complained last night when I let

him bring it into the bedroom.
We were ready to sleep, to read a few
pages out of our novels, then
to flip off the lights. The dog,

not an avid reader, but a thinker,
was ready to chew, to ruminate
on his haunches. Now, he eyes
the vacuum from the bed, its

Hoover motor sucking the night's
bone fragments. Finally, he jumps
down and trots up to my desk,
pronounces a solid growl, coughing

up a bark. I agree the vacuum is an
annoying sound, one of the worst
in homemaking history. I calm
his venting, and he flops at my feet,

smart enough, not to raise
his voice to my wife, vacuuming

in her rose night shirt like Hera
at the hearth. Let us sit here, dog,

in our exile. We have more crumbs,
more bones of poetry to drop. She
will not stop until we are homogenized
like a couple of bottles of milk.

The Story of Masks

Every town has a story, as many
as there are men and women, as many
as there are conflicts of passion, as
many as there are aspirations, resignations,
and acceptances of fate. In them,
we find ourselves, then as much
as now. Nothing is ever new,
not the pain, not the joy,
simply re-varnished, shined up,
written in another tabloid. Check
the stones at our feet, the afternoon
wind turning the leaves, children
playing make believe, dogs baying
at the ancient moon. We are all
nerve synapses, sparking
across visceral gaps, keeping
the body of some giant cognizant,
apprised of the long story, let us say,
in the battle over masks, plague, or
quarantine. Or maybe, we are but
records of breath and body temperature,
sentient in both movement and repose,
to say we are alive is to say
the earth breathes.

Hunting Morels

Janet is swinging a machete
through the thick undergrowth

up near the pond on the family farm.
She remembers a time when she walked

easily to the hill where the morels
surprised them each spring, maybe

for one week, maybe for two, popping
like thumbs from the leaf mold.

There was a time when the trail
seemed clear with her mother in charge.

Now, she leads, canvas satchel at her hip.
With her daughter she fights

the briar, swings the machete through
the tangle of brush, the new briars.

Selling Cannoli

He barely remembers his Sicilian surname,
fat with vowels, sweet on the tongue
like the cannoli his grandfather
makes each Christmas, a family
recipe no doubt, good with coffee,
with predictions of snow.
His grandfather took an Irish name
simpler to explain to spell to keep a job.
Pastries are the history he shares,
his mother in a blue apron, rolls flour tubes,
adds ricotta, egg white, sugar dust.
His grandson sells the cannoli at school, gifts
favorite teachers, his girlfriend's mother.
We buy a dozen for Christmas dinner,
arrange them like a sunburst on a blue plate.

Terminal Blend

Boy in the Spiral Notebook

The boy locked himself in the bathroom
and wrote about planets with two moons,
unrelenting tides, and cities built into cliffs.
His protagonist found hope in puffins.

When a neighbor caught him
fondling another boy in the seat of a Buick,
he feared God, the neighbor from
the same church, from the coffee
and donuts after mass.
He waited for the phone call to his father,
the one he imagined in his spiral notebook,
rehearsing explanations, waiting
until the shop anvil bent him like a fishhook.

The boys parked in a country cemetery
far from town, alone with
coyotes in hedgerows, owls, ghosts.
At night he feared walking in the front door,
expected the lamp next to his father's chair
to snap on like an interrogation bulb.

At the prom he imagined Kathy's
breasts like an absolution,
touching nothing below the waist,
spilling cherry vodka. He danced
to keep the others guessing, buying time
in his best disguise.

Finally Invisible

Three boys in a boat
troll the strip pit's bank.
I sit in the woods
after a walk, watching
the water, the sway of briars
and compass weed,
the insurgence of mined land.
I follow the boys' voices up the pit
towards me. They are
little concerned with fishing, more
with being together, catching
up on the gossip behind
a girl's name, a muscle car.
They hush when passing below me,
raise their faces to the poplars
with the thrashers and nuthatches.
They scan the dump
of sluffed-off tailings, the thickets
hollowed with shadows, each
as if by searching the scrub growth
can find something lost.
The moment smooths, eyes relax,
their conversation a short cast
below willow limbs.

Camouflage

In the trees where the heron nests
the lake water comes to rest, green,
shallow through the cattails.
I paddle slowly up to the bank, nestle
the bow into the branches. Here,
it is finally quiet, the still finger
of a busy lake. The heron squawks,
disgruntled at my interruption.
It is a balancing act where our worlds meet.
I must pay her for my visit by backing
away slowly, careening my neck
for a glimpse of her gray feathers.
We are not so different I want to say,
slipping into the shadow behind the shadows,
watching as the boats speed by, as the jet skis
pirouette in the sun. Our old men
pretend to be young with their Mercury
outboards, cranking their classic rock
as if to hide themselves, green
in the shadow of decibels.

Mudbank Brown

Some days I am moored
like a wooden boat, oars unmanned
inside against the thwarts.
There is little current to move
my weathered mass. Morning
burns away slowly, recedes
into the trees like a possum
in mud. It seems I have little
control of the tethered line,
looped, dipped through
the quiet water. I am always
the stillness in my own wake,
tied to shoreline,
the heavy planks caulked
with hemp and tar, makeshift
with jake-legged buoyancy.
Dragonflies ride the open eyes
of my oarlocks, neither here
nor there. They are sparks
of insight, as bright as wild
crepe myrtle. This is not
depression, as some would claim,
but a type of living imagined
of muskrats and crows.

Pandemic 2021

Our pup eases out of the door
into his first snowstorm
                He searches the wind
with each carefully placed paw

    I'm not wearing my glasses
but he appears to taste the ice pellets
    the flakes
        to breathe the zero
    into his lungs

At my feet
—the potted chrysanthemum rattles

                    with beginning
rather than the end

                .

Final Moth

There's a moth in the ivy this morning,
a white moth held by the early cold.
By all accounts, he should be dying, dead,
or migrating (if moths, like monarchs
migrate). At the least, he should be in a closet,
chewing a hole in a sweater. I nudge him
with my finger, and he moves a step
towards the end of the leaf. Then nothing,

and I'm sure he's taken his last flight, his final
flutter, as moths say of one another at moth wakes
held in the back of someone's
trunk of valuable papers. They speak
in low voices which adds a touch of dignity
to the poem they're eating like a casserole.

Cricket Shoes

There's something out of reach in October
so far beyond me that I cannot put a name to it.
It waits on the path through the trees, the damp leaves
rich with gold and orange, in some cases
the stems standing upright, also bright, also colored.

Thoreau said, the leaves teach us how to die,
but I am not so lucky, for I have learned only to want
more. Even more of the falling, the inaudible gasp
of the leaf letting go from the branch, the brief
twirling as it catches the light, the loosened shoelaces,
the wallered eyelets, the cricket taps its shoes
before the first freeze, the tune singular,
as much laced to earth as tied to hope.

Hardwood Basketball

When my wife slips, locked
in a held ball with the dog, some-
thing inside me falls,
even when she stands, cradling
her wrist, I stay down,
wondering if this is how
the end begins. Muscles
fail to hold. Bones snap.
The heart dribbles slower
until it stops, an arrhythmia
against the gymnasium door.

She tells me to snap out of it.
It's March Madness.
I wipe the baseline with a towel.
Her father used to tell us
not to grow old,
and, of course, we laughed,
agreeing to follow his
advice, and leap for the alley-oop
until the buzzer. But here
we are, more old than young,
worrying about the zone,
the man-on-man, the next
slip on the hardwood.

The Big Gray

I've usually pictured November
as the gray month. That's not meant
to sound negative, since I like gray,

a soothing color, cool to touch, slightly
turned towards the inner voice, the indoors
of long nights, early suppers,

an old movie on Turner, reading
before the lights go out. In November
there is more time for sitting

at the window, watching squirrels
running across the top of the fence,
leaping from roof to limb.

With that thought, I am happy
to drink coffee with nowhere to go,
to forget the noise of bright flowers,

the rush to save, to put up tomatoes
as a symbol, a harvest ritual
if we're ready, if we're lucky.

A Problem with Tomato Sauce

The dog and I share a meatball without sauce.
I would offer him spaghetti, soaked
in good marinara, but he's allergic to tomatoes

like I am predisposed to his dander.
It keeps me up at night while the world sleeps
blowing my nose, folding my handkerchief,

wiping each nostril. The dog, on the other hand,
licks his feet, sometimes whines
as he chews between his toes, scratches his ears.

I'm Italian, giving up spaghetti is out of the question.
The dog a Heinz, rescued
from the side of a Missouri road, survived by

digging through discarded cans and roadkill.
He has never met a meal he didn't admire.
We are both allergic to what we love.

He holds me with his baleful eyes, howls
as I wind my fork with spaghetti noodles.

Garage Storage

A folding metal chair in industrial
brown paint, the yellow stencil
of Brother's Funeral Home

on the back rest, a sparrow's nest
inside a scuffed motorcycle helmet,
grass and string and feather.

A canning jar on the work bench
filled with nuts and bolts,
odd wood screws that once kept

a swing fastened, a glass door sliding
open into the garden. Now, clouded
with dust, a smear of bicycle chain

grease, its blue catches the light,
bells like a gourd,
whittled glass embossed with a name

of a company known for canning,
for storage, for keeping
summer through winter.

Entering the Auction Barn

There's no place left to sit in the auction barn.
One woman has her coat next to her on a chair.
She's either saving it for someone, or keeping it
for herself as a safe space. A man with a wool cap
and a black Patagonia coat comes in out of the cold,
stamps his feet free of last week's snow. He sizes
up the room, the auctioneer's ring worker, holding
a flintlock. The auctioneer chants, hunting
for the first bite. The man, tilts the brim of his cap,
raises his hand. A trio of bids follow.
The man in the Patagonia walks to the woman
and leans to her ear. She moves her coat to her lap.
He slides the chair to the front of the auction barn,
motions to see the rifle. He examines the stock,
the brass lock plate, the frozen trigger. He shakes
his head no, waves it away. The auctioneer
moves on to the back of the barn.
The man unzips his coat, pulls it away from his chest,
and extends his legs easily into the aisle.

Linseed Oil

I paid too much, my neighbor said,
turning the sap bucket, oak staves
golden with linseed rub, blackened

iron ring-bands still tight, ochre rust
below the rivets, smith-hewn iron
hammered into a bale. Yes, old man,

I liked it, too, but I had my own tab
rung up in the auctioneer's chant,
the maybe-Navajo thunderbird

of woven wool, cream fibers, natural
next to the warm aniline red, the
black diamond design, centered

a bit askew. Too much to pay, I said,
for sheep's wool and dye,
too much to render for a bucket

and a rug. We laugh at ourselves,
gray men buying up the past
as quickly as it's forgotten.

Glaucoma

Someday, if the glaucoma wins, will
I hear more than I do today? Will
my ears grow larger, more in tune
to the dog sleeping, the coffee
cooling, the pair of pants laughing
with the mismatched shirt?
When I'm blind,

will I hear what's behind shut doors,
closed windows, the arrangement
of pillows on the couch?

Will I learn the creak of the ash tree?
Will I listen to what's inside
your heart, inside
the one thousand hearts,
embracing, and separating,
and embracing again
like the shadows of branches
under streetlights, drawn, parted,
woven together by the whatever,
or the whomever,
who weaves the wind?

Will my new ears like grandfather's
need more cleaning, more
deep scrubbing? Will I play piano?

Hydrangea

My wife is the gardener, but
she wants me to help her dig a hole
for a new bush she picked up

at the nursery. I'll shovel away
the dirt and sandstone
while she separates the cable

television wire from the roots.
I'll need the axe. She worked
yesterday with a hand spade

and a Boy Scout hatchet. Poor girl.
This is what husbands are for,
especially those who spend the day

with a book on Zen Buddhism,
and then, at night with a Netflix
docuseries on tigers. It's a simple

trade—his back for a shrubbery,

his under-worked hamstrings
for yellow blossoms,
a dead drop for wiffle balls

lost by grandchildren.

Making Sense of Berries

The tall grass, thick with scrub trees
and weeds, is neither
prairie or woods. It's crossed with small
game trails, wallows of late-night deer.
Now that we've had a good freeze,
I can see through the matted grass to the runnels
of field mice and voles. They trail
into thickets snarled with briar,
invested with what I cannot identify.
I need a field guide to pull
out of a coat pocket, a pencil for notes.
                    Naming red berries
is as good a vocation as most,
better than some. Few fall
to fast talking or are swindled by ambition.
Even on the best days, brittle leaves
rattle on stalks. No one is blamed
for the death of leaves. A naturalist
can be as optimistic as a sparrow,
comparing photographs of pokeweed,
keeping a catalogue of what is edible,
                    what is poison.

Terminal Blend

                                        Death is
shelved like a coffee mug in a cabinet,
hidden behind our favorite cups,
the ones that best fit our hands.
We know where it waits, the blue stoneware.
Throughout the days ahead, it is pushed
to the open door, jostled to the front,
though we've tried to avoid
it's thick handle, its empty bowl.
We used to drink bottomless cups
at Harry's Café on Sunday mornings
after Mass. In time, I would
lay my hand over the lip of my cup,
back when plenty was enough.

forgotten in the walnut's
leaves—another bird's
name

Al Ortolani's poetry has appeared in journals such as *Rattle, New York Quarterly*, and *Prairie Schooner*. His most recent collections are *The Taco Boat*, published by New York Quarterly Books in 2022, and *Swimming Shelter* from Spartan Press which was named a Kansas Notable Book for 2021. His novel *Bull in the Ring* was released by Meadowlark Books in 2023. He is a winner of the Rattle Chapbook Prize and has been featured in Garrison Keillor's Writer's Almanac and Ted Kooser's American Life in Poetry. Ortolani recently directed a memoir writing project for Vietnam veterans in association with the Library of Congress and Humanities Kansas. As a retired high school teacher, he enjoys a life without bells and fire drills. He's a sucker for auctions and garage sales. Ortolani is a husband, father, and grandfather, currently entertaining the idea of becoming a hermit.

This project was made possible, in part, by generous support from the Osage Arts Community.

Osage Arts Community provides temporary time, space and support for the creation of new artistic works in a retreat format, serving creative people of all kinds — visual artists, composers, poets, fiction and nonfiction writers. Located on a 152-acre farm in an isolated rural mountainside setting in Central Missouri and bordered by ¾ of a mile of the Gasconade River, OAC provides residencies to those working alone, as well as welcoming collaborative teams, offering living space and workspace in a country environment to emerging and mid-career artists. For more information, visit us at www.osageac.org

Osage Arts Community